DOG

KT-430-898

The author

Dr David Sands

Dr David Sands gained his higher degree in animal behaviour at Liverpool University. He heads the Animal Behaviour Clinic in Chorley, treating problem dogs, cats, exotic birds and horses. He is a practitioner member of the Canine and Feline Behaviour Association and has written numerous books and provided photographs on a range of pets from tropical fish to cats. David has also appeared in a number of pet-related television programmes.

ACKNOWLEDGEMENTS

I would like to thank my family and my clients for introducing me to a wide range of dog breeds as companions. Many generations of my own boxer dogs later, I am a little more informed about the joy of keeping 'man's best friend'. Thanks to Heather for her editorial guidance which helped to correct my literary wanderings.

Dedication

To Caitlin, Faye, Jon, Bob, Matthew and Max who keep me busier than any canine pack.

Family Pet Guides

DOG

Dr DAVID SANDS

First published in 2002 by
HarperCollins*Publishers*
77–85 Fulham Palace Road
Hammersmith
London W6 8JB

The HarperCollins website address is
www.**fire**and**water**.com

Collins is a registered trademark of
HarperCollins Publishers Limited.

07 06 05 04 03 02
9 8 7 6 5 4 3 2 1

A catalogue record of this book is
available from the British Library.

ISBN 0 00 712283 7

THIS BOOK WAS CREATED BY
SP Creative Design for
HarperCollins*Publishers* **Ltd**
EDITOR: Heather Thomas
DESIGN AND PRODUCTION: Rolando Ugolini
PHOTOGRAPHY: Rolando Ugolini,
Bruce Tanner, Charlie Colmer, David
Dalton and Dr David Sands p.35.

ACKNOWLEDGEMENTS
The publishers would like to thank the
following for their kind assistance in
producing this book: Carole Brame and
her dog, Simba; Gregory Rice and his
Springer Spaniel, Gypsy; Steve and
Jennifer Lucas and their Lucas Terriers,
Rugby and Harry; Christine Ugolini and
her Cocker Spaniel, Jasper.

COLOUR REPRODUCTION BY Colourscan,
Singapore
PRINTED AND BOUND BY Printing Express
Ltd, Hong Kong

Contents

Introduction

Dogs are not our whole life but they help make our lives whole.

Roger Caras

Out of all our domesticated companion animals, it is the dog that has adapted to our lifestyles the best. Perhaps it is the strong social structure that the human-canine pack provides. If you add the fact that horses are difficult to accommodate in our living rooms and cats continue to hunt even when offered a habitual food regime, it should come as little surprise that dogs are the pets most suited to be called our best friends. Indeed, 'Man's best friend' has always been a successful working dog or a faithful companion.

Dogs can become the best of companions from many viewpoints. Our domesticated canines listen to our tales of woe and joy with an equally sympathetic ear. They inform us with a bark when the doorbell sounds and guard our homes whilst we are away. Our pet pals are supposed to offer unconditional love, obedience and faithfulness. Without wishing to dispel any popular myths here, all these aspects of keeping a dog will be considered in the following pages.

This book is for individuals and families who have just acquired, or who are considering keeping, a puppy or a dog and need a guide to breed types, and owning and training their pet. Owning a family dog should be a rewarding experience. The information contained within these pages will help ensure that the rewards of companionship are mutually satisfying for both your family and your canine chum.

CHAPTER ONE

Choosing a dog

Choosing a dog is one of the most important decisions you will ever have to make as the dog will become your companion and a member of your family for many years to come. A successful selection will be easier if you assess your lifestyle honestly.

I f you and your family are fit and healthy and are fortunate enough to live in a rural setting, with a large garden and youth and time to spare, then the interactive world of puppies and dog breeds can have few boundaries. Should your home be near to open fields with leafy public footpaths, leading to grazing meadows and tree-lined walks, a dog is now looking for you. And if your family has ample free time for walking and enjoys it in all weathers, then there are few breeds that would prove unsuitable. In contrast, if you are more accustomed to a sedate lifestyle or your home is within a busy urban setting where a green-field walk is streets and major roads away, then some breeds would be incompatible. A working or active 'country' breed would be inappropriate for city life with its expanses of concrete and tarmac.

▌The compatibility factors

An important factor to consider when choosing a dog is whether family members are away from home on each working day. In this situation, it is not a good idea to choose a puppy or one of the large, demanding and athletic breeds. Such dogs usually require plenty of walks and open spaces in which to run and exercise on a regular daily basis. It is important to match the compatibility factors between your family's lifestyle and the breed you wish to keep. For example, huge or boisterous breeds are not suitable for small homes or for owners with a relaxed lifestyle, especially elderly ones. Lively medium to large breeds usually require copious amounts of food, and therefore you must also look at your budget and how much you can afford to pay to feed your dog.

The best breeds to match a small home or a relaxed lifestyle are the toy and miniature dogs, lap dogs, small terrier types and cross-breeds. However, if your family is young and brimming with spare time and energy, any of the working breeds, such as Pointers, Setters, Labradors, Retrievers, Collies and German Shepherds, are also ideal.

Below: *Working dogs like Springer Spaniels need plenty of exercise to become successful members of your family 'pack'.*

The family factor

Few pedigree breeds are ever described in literature as being 'poor with children'. However, many of the so-called 'intelligent breeds' or working dogs, such as German Shepherds, Border Collies, Corgis, Springers and various hounds, can be difficult to manage and are not ideal with children if they are not trained. When they encounter other dogs or livestock or find an exciting scent, these breeds can become oblivious to even the loudest commands.

Above: *Most Terriers are intelligent small dogs and make good pets.*

Many 'working' and 'gundog' breeds also need close handling and must be firmly controlled whilst others have an instinctive need to perform work or agility tasks. Provided that you and your family have the hours to commit to a 'country dog' then there is no reason why 'working breeds' should not be kept successfully in a home environment.

For people with less time and space, the smaller Terriers can make excellent pets for a family living in an urban environment. Provided that these small breeds have inherited a 'good temperament' from their litter mother, they can be easy to train and walk on a lead. Small Terriers require modest amounts of food and can be handled by the smallest of children under parental supervision.

Right: *Although they can make great pets, Boxers may be just too boisterous for some family situations.*

In sharp contrast, large breeds require equally large homes and strong handlers. In the home, a medium- to large-sized dog can often be controlled without difficulty, but outside, especially when attracted to scents, other dogs and distractions, a large, powerful dog can send young members of the family sprawling or pull a lead out of a weak hand and run free. Do consider all these factors before making a decision that you may come to regret.

Hairy or smooth-coated dog?

Most dogs moult, and many leave hairs everywhere although the amount can be reduced through regular grooming with a brush and comb. Whereas long-coated breeds, such as Shih Tzus and some Collies, require daily grooming if their coats are not to become matted, the smooth-coated breeds, such as Dalmatians and Boxers, need less frequent grooming. In addition, some breeds with a wiry coat, such as Airedale Terriers and Poodles,

need to be stripped or clipped once or twice a year, or even every few months if they are to be kept looking neat and tidy. If you do not have much spare time for grooming, it is better to choose a short- or wiry-coated breed. However, if time is not a problem and you enjoy grooming, then you may prefer to own a dog with a longer coat. If so, do remember to check that no members of your family are allergic to dog hairs.

Left: *Breeds such as the Old English Sheepdog need a very high level of grooming. Clipping is often the only way of maintaining their thick coats.*

True breed or mongrel?

Buying a dog

Another factor to consider when choosing between pedigree and mongrel dogs is that the pedigree breeds, especially show dogs, are always expensive whereas mongrels are far more affordable. If you think that you might wish to 'show' your dog at some stage, then you must buy an accredited pedigree animal.

There is an ancient 'urban myth' that mongrels or 'non-pedigree dogs' (cross-breeds and randomly-bred dogs) are tougher and less 'highly strung' than their pedigree cousins and that they need less attention. Whereas it is true that selective breeding will often exaggerate physical and behavioural defects, breeders of pedigree dogs can usually provide a clear picture of the temperament of their animals. Remember that whether a dog is a mongrel or a pedigree, its temperament is always far more important than its looks! The best family dogs, regardless of breed, are friendly, obedient and faithful. Bright eyes and a healthy coat will show the condition of a dog, but it is the way in which it behaves with strangers and other animals that reveals its true worth as a companion. If in doubt, why not consult your local vet who can advise you as to the best breeds to consider and may be able to recommend some accredited local breeders. You could also contact the Kennel Club or The Pet Care Trust for a list of breeders. It is never advisable to buy a puppy without knowing its background, so you should always inspect the breeder's facilities. Nor should you be afraid to ask to see its parents. Seek out family and friends

Left: *A mongrel can be a faithful and amusing friend.*

CHAPTER
ONE

who have breed experience; they can offer you in-depth information and advice. However, bear in mind that breed bias can colour people's opinions.

Right: *Whether it's a mongrel or top-of-the-range pedigree, don't be afraid to give the animal a good check all over. If possible, study its behaviour with people and dogs and see how obedient it is before you buy.*

Pet shops and 'puppy farms'

The pet shop or farm puppy will usually have an unknown past. It may have been removed from the litter mother before the minimum six weeks stage. Some commercial puppy farming is intensive and litters are often moved around; litter mothers can be neglected and 'nesting' conditions are usually entirely unsuitable. The puppies offered in pet shops and commercial farms may also be the result of an unwanted pregnancy where the male dog is unknown and the parental temperaments cannot be guaranteed.

Small pet shops cannot properly accommodate a litter of puppies. If you should encounter 'distressed puppies' in pet shops or farms, it is not advisable to 'rescue' them, however appealing they may be. Instead, advise the appropriate authorities and let them deal with the matter professionally.

Buying a puppy from a working farm or smallholding should also be considered carefully. The parent dogs will often be working or basic guard dogs, and the behaviours that are associated with controlling livestock and protecting property and territory will be accentuated. These behaviours, which are desirable in working dogs, may be unacceptable in a family.

THE MAIN BREED GROUPS

Gundogs

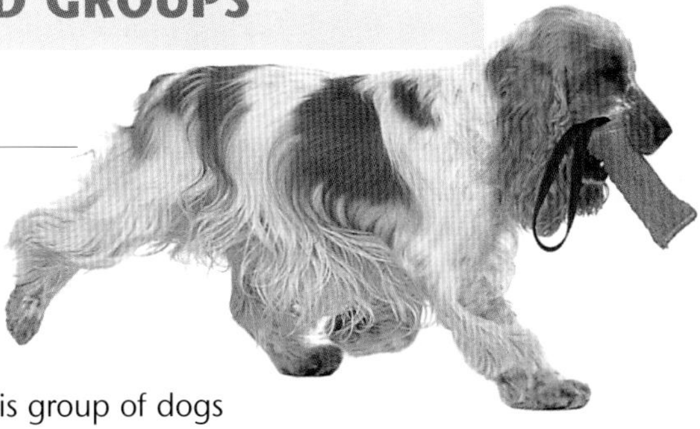

This group includes the Golden Retriever, Labrador Retriever, Setters, Pointers, Weimaraner, and Cocker and Springer Spaniels. In general, this group of dogs is of small to medium size and are considered to possess a happy and intelligent temperament. However, most of these breeds are often happiest when 'working' and they can be prone to hyperactivity and over-dependency problems in the home. This is especially true of puppies bred from working stock or on farms.

These breeds are generally thought to make good family pets, especially Retrievers and Labradors, which are renowned for their gentle and obliging nature.

❖ English Cocker Spaniel

Pet rating

Lifestyle:	Moderate
Exercise:	Demanding
Environment:	Rural
Cost:	Moderate
Grooming:	Easy/moderate

❖ Golden Retrievers

CHAPTER
ONE

▍Working breeds

These include the Boxer, Rough, Shetland and Border Collies, Welsh Corgi, Dobermann Pinscher, German Shepherd Dog, Old English Sheepdog, Briard, Bouvier, Mastiff, Rottweiler, Newfoundland, Great Dane and St Bernard. With the exception of the Corgi (30 cm/12 in tall), the dogs in this group are medium to large in size and require a lot of exercise and close handling. The larger breeds have usually been line-bred for guarding or livestock control. They are extremely strong and, as such, can be very difficult to control in the home and on walks if they are not fully trained in obedience skills.

Pet rating

Lifestyle: Demanding

Exercise: Demanding

Environment: Rural

Cost: Moderate/expensive

Grooming: Moderate/demanding

❖ *Great Dane*

Working dogs are generally known to bond with individuals and are considered to be affectionate and protective towards family members. Because of these attributes, it is important to acquire your puppy from a responsible breeder to ensure that it is also good natured towards people and other animals.

❖ *Border Collie*

Hounds

Basset Hounds, Beagles, Deerhounds, Irish Wolfhounds, Dachshunds, Whippets and Greyhounds all know how to follow a scent until it goes cold, which may mean over hill and vale and miles away from your control. Members of this group can form extremely powerful bonds with individual owners and this can lead to over-dependency. When they are channelling their energies into 'hunting and foraging' walks, these dogs are in bliss. If you have plenty of spare time for walking, then a hound can be the perfect companion. However, long periods spent away from its owner can lead to it becoming withdrawn and unhappy.

❖ Deerhound

❖ Dachshund

❖ Beagle

Pet rating

Lifestyle: Demanding
Exercise: Demanding
Environment: Rural
Cost: Moderate/expensive
Grooming: Easy/moderate

CHAPTER
ONE

Utility group

This category of dogs includes some easily recognised breeds, such as Dalmatians, Bulldogs, Shih Tzus and Poodles. The range of sizes varies dramatically, especially in the Poodle group, which includes small to fairly large dogs. There are varying opinions as to their nature; some, such as smaller Poodles and Dalmatians, can make good family pets, whereas others, such as Bulldogs, can prove to be difficult for children to handle. Poodles were originally line-bred to act as 'in the water' retrievers and thus could be considered as an ex-working breed.

Pet rating

Lifestyle: Moderate

Exercise: Moderate/demanding

Environment: Rural/urban

Cost: Moderate

Grooming: Easy/moderate

❖ *Standard Poodle*

❖ *Dalmatian*

Terriers

This category includes Airedale, Welsh, Border, Wire Fox, Cairn, Jack Russell, Staffordshire, Scottish, Lakeland and West Highland White Terriers. They are generally small, tenacious dogs and are considered to be happy and energetic by nature. This breed group brings together a collection of endearing dogs which are also extremely alert and make excellent watch dogs. Terriers require daily exercise but not as much as the larger working dogs. With firm handling, they can make wonderful family pets.

Pet rating

Lifestyle:	Easy/moderate
Exercise:	Easy/moderate
Environment:	Rural/urban
Cost:	Moderate
Grooming:	Easy/moderate

❖ *Staffordshire Bull Terriers*

❖ *West Highland White Terrier*

❖ *Airedale Terrier puppy*

CHAPTER
ONE

▌Toy companion dogs

This category includes Papillons, Cavalier King Charles Spaniels, Lhasa Apsos, Chihuahuas, Pekingeses, Pugs and Yorkshire Terriers. As the group name suggests, these dogs are small, but their breeders and owners agree that what they lack in stature, they certainly make up for in character. They are usually lively and intelligent, do not require a great amount of exercise but demand a lot of attention from their owners.

❖ *Pug*

❖ *Lhasa Apso*

Pet rating

Lifestyle:	Easy
Exercise:	Easy
Environment:	Urban
Cost:	Economical/moderate
Grooming:	Easy/moderate

❖ *Cavalier King Charles Spaniels*

▌Puppy or adult?

Once you have decided on a pedigree or cross-bred dog, it's time to think about whether to get a puppy or an adult. Most families choosing a pedigree breed select a puppy. At six to eight weeks old, a properly socialized puppy, the offspring of a litter mother with a good temperament, is usually the best choice for an active family and, with the correct handling, will become a fully integrated member. Puppies are quick to learn, fast to train and grow up knowing 'where they belong' in the human-canine pack. They need to be house-trained, although the litter mother starts this process.

Above: *A Yorkshire Terrier puppy and adult dog. You must consider what you want; puppies are easier to train.*

A dog or a bitch?

Choosing which sex can be difficult. Discuss this with the breeder who will take into account your personal situation and needs. Male dogs may want to roam more freely than bitches (female), but they do not come into 'season' – the time when bitches are 'on heat' and ready to breed. At these times, bitches need to be isolated from any males to prevent unplanned matings. Females are said to be more reliable, less aggressive and more home loving although this varies from breed to breed.

Male dogs instinctively want to 'scent and mark' their territory, through urine and faeces, and to 'over-mark' the territory of other dogs. In contrast, bitches are less inclined to scent and behave in this manner. It is possible for a bitch to be dominant amongst dogs of different sexes, but often it is the male dog that feels the need to show aggression and challenge in order to ascertain its place in the human-canine pack (family).

CHAPTER
ONE

Above: *Deciding on which puppy to buy will depend partly on observation of the puppy's behaviour and personal preference.*

Puppy selection

Selecting the best out of a litter of beautiful, cuddly puppies is not always as straightforward as it may sound. Should you pick the largest, liveliest individual – the 'pick of the litter' – or the shy 'runt of the litter'? This is a difficult question. Without background information on the breeds involved and their temperament, puppy selection is almost a lottery. But the same gamble can exist whether you buy a mongrel or a pedigree puppy. Even though you may see the mother with her puppies, the father's temperament cannot always be observed and confirmed.

Try to observe your 'target' puppy in its active moments. All sleeping puppies appear to be 'angels'. Sometimes it is wiser to choose a puppy that is neither extrovert – 'boisterous' – or withdrawn and introverted. It may be wise to select the canine equivalent of 'Mr Average'. The same strategy can be used when selecting an adult dog. Don't choose your pet when it is sleeping and try to avoid the most excitable or the quietest animal. Look for one that shows some calmness.

Adult dog selection

If you are choosing an adult dog, don't be afraid to ask if you can take the dog on a lead walk to test its initial obedience and general responsiveness. If the dog will not respond to basic 'stop' and 'sit' commands, there is a strong possibility that you and your family will have a challenge. If dog training is your forte, however, then disobedience will not deter you from the animal of your choice. To achieve a smooth, gentle integration into your family, it is better to choose a quiet, biddable dog rather than a lively, uncontrollable and difficult-on-the-lead type one.

Young puppies chew in the teething period, and although this can create some temporary handling problems, they can be overcome by careful control. However, an adult dog who is destructive or chewing excessively is seeking relief from an emotional disturbance. These dogs, usually from a rescue or re-homing centre, can bring an 'unknown past' into your home. They do not know why they have been 'rejected' by their existing pack – indeed, this 'rejection' can occur several times – and they sometimes struggle to find their place within your new pack. If your family is home-loving and there is always someone around during the day and at weekends, a rescue or re-homed dog can be ideal.

Right: *It is a good idea to take your prospective future companion for a walk to see how he reacts and behaves.*

CHAPTER
ONE

▌ To the rescue

Rescue centres exist to find good homes for dogs that have been abandoned or whose owners can no longer keep them due to family breakup, death, illness or relocation. Large establishments can offer expertise and a certain amount of guidance whereas smaller centres and breed specialists can give specific advice and owner-dog matching skills.

Vetting

Be prepared to answer any questions asked about your lifestyle. They are not being nosey; they genuinely need to know whether you are well equipped to offer a happy home to their dog and whether you will be well suited to each other.

Neutering

Dogs and puppies are also offered to 'good homes' in local newspaper and shop advertisements. Whatever the source of a 'rescued' or 're-homed' dog, it is vital that it should be neutered if it is older than six months – a bitch should be spayed; a male dog castrated. This will prevent any unnecessary or accidental breeding should your new pet come into contact with other dogs. Your vet can advise about this standard surgical operation. However, castration does not eradicate aggression in males and should not be seen as a solution for behavioural problems. It has been suggested that male dogs will cease 'wandering' if they are castrated, and there may be an element of truth in this argument.

Selecting a rescue dog

Making the correct selection as you walk along a line of kennel pens can easily become subjective. A dog with 'pick-me-eyes' may catch your attention first; it may remind you of a previous pet or may demonstrate an appealing aspect of its character. Meanwhile, the general noise and barking may be deafening as some extrovert dogs race to the front, scrambling for attention and hoping to be greeted or fed. More withdrawn and shy dogs may remain curled up and ignore you.

If you are attracted to a particular dog, ask whether you can take it for a walk (further than just around the compound). Don't worry if it appears to be hyperactive when it is put on a lead – this is normal. Your physical contact and the potential for a walk is, apart from food, probably all that a rescue dog 'dreams about'.

Find out about its background (often unknown or sketchy) and how it behaves with other dogs. Some rescue dogs might have been attacked by other dogs and these events can lead to a 'get-in-first' type of fear aggression.

If you are selecting a puppy from a 'rescue litter', the term 'pot luck' may spring to mind. You could try to seek out the average puppy – one that is not biting (although a puppy needs to do this) and not listless. However, bright eyes and a shiny nose will do. It may even be that the puppy picks you!

Left: *A rescue dog, whether it's a cross-breed or a pedigree, can become a much-loved family member and a life-long companion.*

CHAPTER TWO

Understanding your dog

The canine family group includes Foxes, Bush dogs, Painted dogs, Wolves, Dingos, Jackals and a species that represents all our domesticated breeds: Canis familiaris.

A ll the canines, including domesticated pet dogs, have common physical characteristics. These include long jaws and rows of developed teeth. It is these 'flesh ripping', extremely adaptable teeth, permanent in the adult dog, that give the canines their name.

Wild dogs were tamed and crossed with wolves and then man began to make deliberate 'breed selections' for size and coat type for particular working purposes, such as hunting, guarding, pulling sledges and livestock control. In recent centuries, a number of smaller breeds have been developed to serve as companion lap dogs. In addition to our selection, there is a natural influence depending on a breed's geographical origin.

All of the several hundred modern-day dog breeds are identified as belonging to the single species Canis familiaris. Continual line-breeding and cross-breeding, with the species from the wolverine group, were the first important steps in the development of the multitude of breeds we recognise today. Selective breeding has provided us with pets which can live within our homes and accept our family social structure.

CHAPTER
TWO

Wild dogs and man

Dogs were first tamed by early humans. Wild dogs infiltrated human settlements as they scavenged for food. At some point, cubs, taken from adult animals, were kept as a future food source and if these youngsters did not display 'fear' towards their human keepers they became the first companion animals.

Early humans probably used these pre-domesticated dogs to help them hunt prey. As a secondary aspect of a developing relationship, these 'feral dogs' may have also proved useful in guarding early settlements from animal and human invaders.

From those primitive days, after 2,000 years of selective breeding of wild species, such as the grey wolf and jackal, man has produced the wonderful variety of breeds available today.

Top dog

The majority of a dog's behaviour is 'instinctive' and is passed on, genetically, from parent dogs to their offspring. The exact percentages between instinctive (inherited) and learned behaviour are not available because statistically-proven research does not exist. The precise figures may depend on the breed being considered and which expert opinion is followed. Most behaviourists agree that, whilst the greatest percentage of dog behaviour is instinctive, it is the 'learned behaviour' that can be directly linked to behavioural problems. This can be expressed as nervousness or aggression in the home and on walks.

Dogs communicate their position within a pack in nature through the giving or withholding of physical contact and attention. A 'top dog' will show a tendency to ignore all but his mate and will quickly deal with any challengers. The 'challenged' must always hope that the 'challenger' will back down. It is counter-productive for individuals within the pack to 'attack' or

Females

It is a myth that the 'top dog' or alpha is always the male. Females have high status in nature and it is possible, in smaller packs, for an alpha female to act as leader. Research has shown that the second-level females, known as beta females, have a higher status than beta males and cooperate with each other when it comes to cub-caring. Female 'status' probably has its roots in the importance of cub development.

show 'predatory' (wounding or killing) aggression to members within it. Instead, there are 'posturing' behaviours to prevent injury, because in nature true aggression would result in fatalities.

A submissive dog will concede to its superiors; it will not confront them or attempt to take food before them. It will signal its lower position by allowing a dominant dog to stand over it whilst it lies down.

'Pack behaviour', however, is about cooperation. By working together, the pack can hunt large prey. This is why there is support for a hierarchy and

Below: *Siberian Huskies are pack animals, working together in a team.*

leadership – the alpha individuals. 'Top dog' status is shown by who feeds first, who has priority in mate selection and who has the best position in the den area.

❚ Body language

Body language in dogs has evolved to encourage sociability and to counter the need for physical aggression. This form of communication replaces aggression with behaviours that reveal superiority or inferiority.

■ A high status is shown when a dog is standing erect – tail and head up – by raising fur, standing over another, looking for eye contact and holding ground in a dispute.

■ Showing inferiority is just the opposite. This includes rolling over to expose a vulnerable area and mouth licking to show appeasement. These methods of signalling dominance or submissiveness, as used amongst packs of wild canines, are also shown by domesticated dogs.

Left: *Dogs, such as this Siberian Husky, signal submission to their pack leader by licking his mouth.*

Dogs in domestication

Today, we have modified dog behaviour so they can accept us as 'pack leaders – for more information on how you can establish yourself as pack leader, turn to page 39. In the absence of the 'pack', it is our family structure that takes on this form. Dogs cannot see what we can see – that 'they are dogs and we are humans'. In the absence of that knowledge, they accept us as dogs and the human-canine pack is formed.

In the wild, at least half of the time and behaviour of the pack is used up in hunting and foraging. Unlike cats, very few domesticated dogs leave home and 'hunt to make a kill'. Dogs most likely accept that humans provide the 'kill', which may arrive in supermarket bags, and they consider walks with us to be about exploring and scent marking.

Domestication for dogs is about modifying their behaviour to a new set of rules. However, a pair of Border Collies, working together to round up sheep, display similar behaviour patterns to those of Arctic wolves hunting Caribou. This is an example of instinctive behaviour. Both can be seen to display standard 'hunting behaviours', such as circling, dropping down and edging forwards, belly down, to close in on sheep or prey. For wolves, it is the final act of predatory aggression – the kill that will feed the pack – rather than 'rounding up'.

Right: *Many dogs display submissive behaviour towards their human owners by rolling over on their backs to be fussed.*

CHAPTER
TWO

Breed types

Nowadays, domesticated dogs, such as Labrador Retrievers, are trained to act as 'eyes' for the blind; Huskies pull sledges; Spaniels search for drugs or weapons; German

❖ *Boxer*

Shepherds track criminals; and St Bernards and Newfoundlands are used to rescue people from mountains and lakes. As already established, most dog breeds have been developed for size and behaviour with priority for a particular task or characteristic.

■ **A gundog**, such as a Springer Spaniel, has a waterproof coat, keen eyes and a long nose to enhance a strong sense of smell.

■ **Dogs bred for herding and guarding** are strong, sometimes physically squat or low in stance and often short-haired. Picture a Boxer dog: it has powerful, muscular front and hind legs.

■ **Sheepdogs** are leaner and are often long-haired for protection against the cold. They are lightweight – fast enough to enable them to quickly round up sheep. Their 'circle and round up' behaviour has been selectively bred over many centuries.

❖ *German Shepherd*

■ **Packs of hounds**, such as Beagles, which are used for hunting modest-sized animals or flushing and retrieving birds, are often small with short legs, a deep chest, sturdy tail and strong head.

■ **Racing dogs** tend to be sleek, fine-boned, short-haired, with elongated legs and a long head and neck.

■ **Mountain dogs**, used to rescue people in extreme conditions, are usually massive, big-boned with a large head and thick coat.

■ **Northern climate dogs**, which were developed to pull sledges, have deep, luxurious coats to keep out the cold. They can even provide warmth for their keepers.

■ **Many diminutive breeds**, such as the Jack Russell and other small Terriers, were developed to hunt rodents or to flush out target prey from burrows or holes. They have tenacious personalities and active traits. Line-breeding usually means that the larger the Terrier, the bigger the target prey.

Above: *It is instinctive to dig out rodents for Jack Russells and other Terriers.*

■ **The big game hunters** are typically strong and lanky dogs like Great Danes and Rhodesian Ridgebacks. The latter were once used in packs to hunt down lions.

■ **Many of the 'lap dogs' and 'watch dogs'**, such as the Pekingese, Cavalier King Charles Spaniel and Shih Tzu, are miniature which makes them easy to carry around. They can be very vocal and their bark is intended to act as an audible warning of approaching strangers. Their personalities encourage them to form close bonds with their human owners.

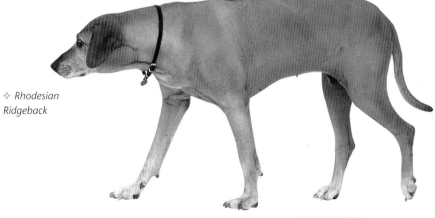

❖ *Rhodesian Ridgeback*

CHAPTER
TWO

Early experience and behaviour

A puppy's earliest experiences will have a significant influence on long-term behaviour and temperament. The first 10 weeks of its life are critical as regards socialization. A litter mother cares for and controls all her pups. She dictates when and how much they can feed from her. She can gently but firmly put her puppies 'in their place' when their behaviour becomes too demanding. She signals, especially in the first three weeks of development (the reflex period), where to toilet, offers them warmth and comfort, and returns wandering individuals to the litter if they explore too far, too early. The pups are kept under her watchful supervision until it is time to allow them independence at five to six weeks.

Faulty learning

Territory, food, protection, warmth and sibling interaction are the essential elements in the natural psychological development of dogs. When a puppy is removed from the litter before six weeks, it will miss out on some aspects of its natural socialization. This is how faulty learning behaviour develops. Interrupted socialization or a poor litter mother can mean a dog will be more nervous and difficult to house-train. It may also result in a dog that continually barks for attention and has a poor temperament.

In its developing 'nervousness', a poorly socialized pup often makes a powerful attachment to one family member. Once this bond has formed, it can quickly become

Left: *A well-adjusted dog is willing to please and has usually had the benefit of good socialization in its early life.*

over-dependent on that person and may 'pine' in their absence.
If it has an inherited dominant characteristic or a poor
temperament, it may become a problem dog. Poor behaviour
can even result in a dog being abandoned or re-housed. In
contrast, a puppy that has been correctly socialized at the litter
stage will display all of the normal developing behaviour we
expect from a youngster. He will form a happy, outgoing
personality and be straightforward to train.

▌How dogs communicate and learn

The first obvious evidence of canine communication you may
notice involves your puppy's tail. This part of the body will move
vigorously from side to side or even in a circle to display that
he is very pleased to see you. In play, he will also offer friendly
behavioural signs, including bowing, pawing, jumping and
pouncing, to encourage you to take part.

    If a stranger comes to the door,
your maturing puppy's coat will
stand up and thicken around the
neck and back and his tail will rise.
Most dogs then bark to signal an
alert. This bark is to advise the
'human-canine pack' that there is a
threat to the inner territory (your
home) and to warn off potential
intruders. All dogs want to help
protect their home territory.

Right: *Some dogs guard their
home territory enthusiastically
and may be over-aggressive towards
strangers, barking and growling.*

CHAPTER
TWO

Canine sounds

Your dog can bark, growl, howl, whine and yelp. These sounds are the simplest aspects of canine language. Dogs have an 'innate sense' of social awareness which stems from the pack life of their ancestors. This 'genetic programming', although diluted over hundreds of years, is a major factor in helping them adapt to a human family structure.

The sounds your dog listens for relate to his own vocal range.

- **The mid-range** is a bark for alert.
- **A low range** is a growl for a challenge (in play and aggression).
- **An upper tone** is a yelp or whine to submit or beg food or contact.
- **A howl**, to communicate at a distance, goes through the whole sound range.

When a dog howls in the home, especially when his owners are absent, it is a sign of separation problems. In effect, the howling dog is calling for his pack members to return.

Dog vocal language

- **A bark** is an alert response, warning of predators or prey.
- **A growl** is a challenge (in play and in aggression).
- **A howl** is a call to a 'pack member' outside visual contact.
- **A whine** is submissive or begging.
- **A yelp** is due to submission, injury or a plea to stop aggression.

Body talk

Dogs can communicate with each other by other methods in additional to vocal sounds. The main method of signalling both status and mood is through body language.

- **A dominant dog** will stand upright, with his ears forwards and tail held straight out. In addition, this dog-type will ruffle up his neck and back hairs, curl his lips and show teeth and make direct eye contact with another dog.
- **A submissive dog**, in contrast, will reply by crouching (bottom down) and by keeping his tail down or by swinging it from side to side. This submissive type, if he doesn't want to challenge, will look away and sometimes lie down and turn over in a submissive

display. The most extreme display of submissiveness in dogs is when its vulnerable underbelly is shown.

These same behaviours can be shown to owners. Dogs perceive humans in the family as a part of the 'pack' as they look for their status within the family. A challenging dog will growl or bark at a family member over food or a toy. He will attempt to compete when going through doors and crossing thresholds. A submissive dog will bow down at every opportunity and will be happy to 'roll over' and show inferiority.

Above: *The Yorkshire Terrier on the left is dominant with its head and ears up as the more submissive dog on the right lowers his head and avoids any eye contact.*

Common scent

In addition to physical and vocal communication, all dogs utilize hormones, pheromones and scents in order to communicate special information. They do not approach each other and vocally 'ask' questions about gender, oestrus cycle or mood. This information is scented by dogs, just as it was between primitive humans. Dogs that are not displaying dominance or aggression will lick each other's mouths to exchange body scents, and sniff each other's bottoms to extract information provided by anal and sexual glands.

They will lick each other in mutual grooming (allogrooming), which originates from the reflex stage when cubs are licked by the litter mother. Another source for this behaviour is when cubs beg for food to be regurgitated. When your dog wants to lick you, it is not a 'kiss' but a method of extracting information about you.

The combination of sound, body and chemical language is a method of communicating which enables dogs to exchange information in order to reduce any potential misunderstandings. In the human-canine pack, they communicate how a dog feels about someone, something or another animal. Although your dog cannot speak the same language as you, it is important to acknowledge that through the 'language of the body and chemical signals', he can communicate far more than we might at first imagine.

How to communicate with your dog

Keep communication with your puppy as simple as possible. Word commands, such as 'sit', 'stay', 'down', 'wait', 'heel', 'walk on' and 'here', can be accompanied with appropriate hand signals or, in the case of recall, with a whistle.

Below: *When dogs meet, they sniff and lick each other to extract information and to communicate with one another.*

If you shout instructions, you might as well have a barking competition. Dogs have sensitive hearing and a loud voice becomes distorted into a kind of bark. Your tone of voice should always be low and firm. Reassure your dog in a kind, upbeat tone.

Signalling your status

In 'dog whispering' terms, you can signal your status to your pet. Offer attention on your terms; not the other way round.

■ Go through doorways first and eat first. Even if you are not ready to eat, be demonstrative and eat a slice of toast in front of your puppy before feeding him.

■ Apply psychological, rather than physical, control on walks. If your puppy pulls, tell him to stop and sit before proceeding. He will soon learn that pulling means stop but behaving means going forwards.

■ Do not encourage him to sit or lie on furniture. On the same level, he can use the situation to attempt to elevate his status over yours.

■ He should not sleep with you unless you are prepared to concede status and run the risk of over-dependency.

■ The contrast between your presence and absence can be extreme if your dog has complete and continual access to you when you are at home. It is important to encourage him to be independent and confident. There should be times when you

Right: *Discourage your dog from climbing up on sofas, chairs and beds. He should be on a lower level.*

are separated from him, even though you are home. Periods of separation should include overnight and hourly sessions during evenings and at weekends.

▌ Nervous and aggressive behaviours

When treating their animals as human companions – known as anthropomorphizing – owners can encourage antisocial behaviours. 'Humanizing' your puppy or dog can lead to a wide range of behavioural problems, such as aggression, insecurity, distress, destructiveness and over-dependency. However, it is possible for us to display control and dominance over a 'status-seeking' dog (looking for his place in the pack) in a positive, non-aggressive way.

There is a great deal of confusion linked to the idea of humans expressing dominance and control over a dog. The correct understanding and subsequent application of these factors will not cause a dog to be cowed and fearful. It is not necessary to shout at or strike a dog to express owner-control or to show an animal that it must respond to instructions. When handling problems occur, loud and aggressive reactions will immediately increase

▌ **Left:** *It's easy to give confusing signals about a dog's status in its human 'pack'. The black Labrador obviously isn't happy!*

distress in a dog and often reinforce nervous behaviour.

If a puppy is exposed to positive training from the beginning (a stroke, a pat, praise and/or a food treat for good behaviour), he will be eager to learn. When he has positively responded to an instruction to sit, stay or recall and he is rewarded, then this behaviour will be encouraged. Adult dogs can often be re-trained with nothing more than a simple food-reward system.

Above: *Regular and consistent puppy training will help ensure a happy and obedient adult dog who will adapt well to family life.*

Fear and territorial aggression

Happy dogs don't bare their teeth, hide under tables or chase livestock. 'Fear aggression' develops from experiences in which a dog is attacked by other dogs or mistreated in some way. 'Fear' is adrenalin-driven and can make a nervous dog charge at the door when letters are delivered. The postman leaves immediately so the dog thinks he has won the confrontation and gains relief from the perceived success. Thus territorial and fear aggression can become addictive. Dogs who display 'fear aggression' may develop a 'get in first' syndrome of behaviour. They attack because they perceive that they are about to be attacked, but if their owners show 'leadership', this behaviour can be eradicated.

When a dog resorts to 'flight or fight', its nervousness and experience force it back to basic instinct. However, if it is shown consistency and kindness by its owner, it will respond positively. Problem behaviours can be promoted simply by your attention and frustration. It is better to promote good behaviour with attention and ensure your reaction is consistent.

CHAPTER THREE

Looking after your puppy

A positive start in the first months of your puppy's life can make a significant difference to his personality in maturity. By providing for his needs, you can be sure to have a happy, healthy puppy that will be a pleasure to keep.

Ideally, the puppy you choose should not be more than 10 weeks and not less than six weeks old when taken from its litter. If it is younger than six weeks, it will not be socialized and important social skills, including play and feeding, may not be sufficiently developed. These are learned through general interaction with its mother and littermates. Any reduction in the natural development of a dog in its early stages of life can lead to antisocial behaviour as it develops into a mature animal. Alternatively, a puppy that is removed from the litter when it is older than 10 weeks will have developed some dependancy with the litter mother and its human family, and when this attachment is broken its personality may be affected.

CHAPTER
THREE

Bringing your puppy home

When collecting your puppy, ask the breeder for a diet sheet as a guide to feeding. It is best to continue offering the same food for at least a few days while the puppy is settling in. Do your best to create the minimum amount of fuss with your chosen puppy. You might think that it is best to transport your puppy wrapped in a blanket on your knee. However, it is advisable to use a purpose-built wire or plastic formed carrier or an economical cardboard one which can be obtained from pet shops. Safety and security are vital during the first journeys your puppy makes in a car. Arrange for someone to drive you to the breeder so that you can concentrate solely on the needs of the puppy on the way home. Always carry some tissues or kitchen roll just in case the puppy is travel sick.

Equipment

Your new-found friend will require a few items of basic equipment. You can buy these in advance in readiness for his arrival. You will need the following:

■ A pre-formed plastic bed or an old cardboard box to act as a temporary 'basket' while your puppy is chewing
■ Some washable 'vet-bed' or other bedding
■ Solid feeding and drinking bowls, preferably stainless steel or durable plastic
■ Some strong toys, e.g. a strong rubber ball, a durable frisbee or training dummy
■ A puppy collar and short lead – the right length between the puppy's neck when standing and your upright stance
■ Brush and comb for grooming
■ Lots of newspapers for 'house training'.

First night blues

Once you have your puppy safe at home the fun really starts. The first night will probably be the most difficult for him. Few puppies settle down immediately and there could be some crying or even howling – their new life and home are a long way from the familiarity of their mother and littermates. Do not make too much of a fuss of your puppy or pay him excessive attention in this phase or you may unwittingly encourage more of this behaviour in the future. Once you are able to reassure your puppy that he need only ask for love and kindness, he will soon forget the old scramble for his mother's milk and fully adopt his new family.

Beds and crates

A cosy bed on the floor, not too large but big enough to be comfortable and to prevent cold draughts, together with a blanket or some washable 'vet bed', will soon make your puppy feel settled. Better still, a folding travel crate with a cover is perfect to confine and calm your puppy, although a larger bed or crate may be required when your puppy has grown.

It is important that your puppy has a place to rest where he can feel secure. Many dog breeders and dog 'show' people use covered crating as a means to keep a dog secure and quiet. The crate should

Left: *A safe, cosy place for a dog to call its own is essential. A basket should be placed in a quiet location in the home. It should be off limits to children who are often fascinated by sleeping dogs.*

CHAPTER
THREE

Settling in

At first your puppy will want to investigate your house, room by room. Everywhere will be new to your puppy as will the smells and people. Try and protect him from too much fuss and confusion. All your family and friends will want to stroke and cuddle him but sometimes you have to put his welfare first.

Always provide a clean bowl of water and make sure that it is available at all times. However, only put the food dish down at meal times – not in between. Your dog will soon realise that when you bring the dish it is time to eat.

be just large enough to enable the puppy to stand and lie down, with allowance for 12 months' growth. This unit can be used by the puppy to sleep in overnight and for several 30–60-minute rest periods during the day. It is important to teach your puppy to be independent and happy when he is alone and away from the family.

The floor of the crate or travel cage should be lined with a washable fleece or an old item of clothing (your scent will help your puppy to feel secure), and a water bottle (as used for rabbit hutches, etc.) can be added. Allow your puppy to explore this unit for a few days before closing the door.

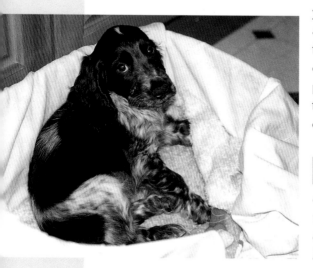

Left: *If your puppy likes to chew, and most do, a cardboard box covered with a blanket or some cosy 'vet bed' makes an ideal temporary bed.*

House-training

As soon as you arrive home with your new friend, offer him the chance to go to the toilet in the garden. If it is really cold and wet, you could encourage him to use the central spot on a spread of newspapers, but it is preferable to venture outside whatever the weather and start off as you mean to go on.

If using newspapers inside, praise your puppy when he uses them. Ignore it if he soils on any other surface inside the home. Only clean up a 'mess' when your puppy is not in view to reduce any potential reinforcement of the behaviour. It is a good idea to put the cleaned-up faeces or mopped urine (with a kitchen roll) in a particular place in the garden. Take your puppy to this spot and show him the 'correct' place to toilet. Eventually, you can reduce indoor newspapers to one at the back door, and this can be removed altogether when the dog learns to go outside.

Remember to take your puppy outside first thing in the morning, after every meal or drink, after exuberant play sessions and when he wakes up from a sleep. These are the times at which he is most likely to want to urinate or defecate. Praise him when he performs and he will soon learn to associate the required action with your praise.

Above: *Always take your dog outside to toilet after eating, and establish a pattern.*

Interacting with your puppy

Puppies have several bursts of energy followed by resting periods throughout the day. In the active periods, they love to chew, but sometimes they target the wrong items. Offer hide or natural bone chews but do not interact with these items. Your puppy may want you to challenge for them (in a game), but this behaviour can lead to possessive aggression.

**CHAPTER
THREE**

You can play retrieve and reward games together with some special hard toys. Keep these interactive toys, such as a ball or small frisbee, in a box so that you can signal when short play sessions are about to commence. It is better to have six short five-minute play sessions over the period of a day than one 30-minute session during which the puppy can become hyperactive and over-stimulated. If you puppy brings you something and drops it at your feet, quickly reward him with praise and a stroke and a small food treat.

Reinforcing good behaviour

If your puppy bites your hands or feet, say 'No' firmly but in a low tone voice – do not shout – and break off from play. He will quickly learn that good behaviour has its rewards whereas antisocial behaviour has none. In this manner, you will reinforce and encourage good behaviour.

Avoiding dominance conflicts

Don't encourage your puppy to climb the stairs or sleep on your bed or furniture as this could create over-dependency or, as the dog grows older, problems relating to the shedding of hairs or being disobedient. A children's stair gate will prevent your puppy going upstairs. Height is an important factor in controlling a dog, and your bed or the stairs can soon be mistaken for a position of importance!

Find the food games

You can play a game of 'search for the food' (a hunting and foraging game). Hide a small food treat in the room or garden away from your puppy. Sound a 'reward whistle' and tell him to seek out the food. This game can progress from a simple start of one treat and an easy location to variations with several treats and more difficult hiding places.

Grooming and care

It is a good idea to groom your puppy every day to encourage a positive association with grooming from the earliest possible age. However, keep the sessions short and sweet to prevent him becoming bored and restless. You can also use this time together to check his general health.

■ Use a soft but firm brush to gently brush his coat and underbelly in a quick session.

■ You may need to follow this brushing with a comb if your puppy is a long-haired breed. **Note:** Place a white or dark towel or cloth, depending on coat colour, underneath your puppy to catch any foreign objects that could warn of flea infestations.

■ Reward good behaviour with a treat, especially if he sits or stands obediently while he is groomed.

Above: *From an early age, get your puppy used to being groomed regularly with a soft brush and comb.*

Above: *Gently comb the ears and long hair, teasing out tangles with your fingers or a comb.*

Left: *A grooming mit is an easy way to groom your puppy. Most dogs love the attention and will sit still.*

CHAPTER
THREE

Health check

After grooming, carefully check your puppy all over, looking for tell-tale warning signs of health problems.

1 Look carefully into the mouth and check the teeth.

2 Check the eyes, ears and nose for any discharge, and wipe these carefully with a damp cloth.

3 Check the puppy's anal area for any signs of sloppy faeces.

4 Check the coat for fleas – these will look like specks of coal dust in the fur.

If you notice anything unusual, talk to your vet. Your puppy will quickly grow to accept this examination and grooming session as part of your relationship.

Visiting the vet

Get the vet to examine your new puppy as soon as possible. He will need essential inoculations, including parvovirus, distemper and leptospirosis. The first vaccination will usually be at between 10 and 12 weeks, followed by a booster two weeks later. Your puppy can't walk in a public place until 10 days after the vaccinations are completed.

The early detection of any physical problems can result in prompt treatment for your puppy. After an inspection, the vet should be able to give him a 'clean bill of health' and offer you advice on worming and flea treatments.

Socialization

Once your puppy has been fully vaccinated against the common canine infections, it is advisable to socialize him. Many veterinary clinics hold classes for puppies that have been vaccinated. These sessions allow you to introduce your puppy to others in a controlled environment and to make sure he does not display any hyperactivity or aggression towards other dogs. Puppy classes are an opportunity to learn more about caring for your dog. The veterinary nurses can offer advice and answer your questions.

You can progress from these introductory sessions to socialization classes with older dogs where basic obedience training and control can be gradually implemented. Your local veterinary clinic can usually advise you on the puppy classes and training schools that are available in your area.

Socializing your puppy
Embark on a socialization programme at home by introducing your puppy to a friendly dog, preferably a known dog because other dogs may not be friendly or may appear so at first and then display

Below: *Puppies can be very persistent and get themselves into trouble at times, even with placid adult dogs.*

Below: *These two are still playing but things could get out of hand. It is best to break them up with an alternative game.*

aggression. Find a neutral walk that is new to both dogs and encourage recall and lead obedience (short, well-rewarded sessions) when both dogs have been successfully introduced.

Avoid excessive competition between your puppy and the other dog, especially in retrieval, because over-competitiveness can sometimes promote aggression. Gentle recall or retrieval is best; as one dog is sent off to retrieve, send your puppy off in another direction. Always end on a positive note with a food treat for an obedient recall. Don't encourage any behaviour that may be a problem when your puppy grows up, such as jumping up or barking excessively. If these behaviours are shown, tell him to sit and offer a food treat – clicker training (see page 86) is excellent for this and will promote 'controlled' behaviour.

Pet pals

Healthy, happy puppies will usually mix happily with almost any animal because they are more adaptable than adult dogs – their associations with many aspects of everyday life have not yet been formed. In the early months of life, there is a natural curiosity between animals which does not encourage aggression.

Dogs that have lived in other homes or during an extended period with a breeder may be more difficult to establish in a new home with an existing animal. To some extent, this is dependent on the dog's breed and age. Older dogs, especially those that have been encouraged to chase cats out of their gardens, will show aggression towards all cats. Sometimes a dog may be friendly towards your own cat but chase others; this has more to do with territory protection than aggression.

Introducing a new puppy to an older dog must be undertaken carefully and slowly even though few happy, healthy adult dogs will show aggression towards a puppy. An existing dog will consider your home to be its territory and therefore to be defended, so introduce him to your new pet in the garden or on some neutral ground nearby.

Discourage any aggression from your existing pet. When introducing an older dog to a younger one, encourage them to play or exercise together in an activity that they can both enjoy. Keep all food well away from them at this initial meeting, and feed separately during the first few days. Only when there is full acceptance of the newcomer by the existing pet can meals be offered in separate dishes at the same time.

Below: *When introducing your new puppy to other dogs, supervise the initial meetings carefully.*

CHAPTER FOUR

The adult dog

Your puppy will develop into a mature adult dog somewhere between 12 and 18 months of age. At this point his physical and hormonal development will have peaked and, in the wild, he would be establishing his place within the pack.

A dult dogs will 'cock' their legs on walks – 'marking' lamp posts and trees – whereas bitches will continue to squat like a puppy. Your dog may challenge you in play sessions or on walks – tugging on the lead or running away from you when he is called. You may notice changes in the proportion of the head to the body and even differences in the thickness and colouring of his coat.

Unlike a puppy, your adult dog should not be mouthing or soft play biting your hands, and he should accept your instructions. He should not be pawing you or barking to demand attention. He should recall at the sound of his name and be able to walk by your side on the lead without excessive pulling.

| Feeding

A young, active adult dog would normally be fed once daily. It is best that this meal is offered after the main walk of the day so

CHAPTER
FOUR

that the dog can rest, digest and absorb his food. Elderly dogs need a lower-protein diet, less food and shorter walks because they are less active than younger dogs. The amount of food your dog requires will not only depend on his age and size but on his activity levels. If he is young and has a lot of exercise, he will need more food than an older dog that prefers to rest.

All dogs require a balanced diet which includes vitamins, proteins, minerals and fibre or roughage. Young dogs require more protein than older dogs because, in the main, they are more active and need protein for growth and carbohydrates for energy. Small to medium breeds weighing between 2–25 kg (4–55 lb), such as Jack Russells and Collies, are known to have between 10–50 per cent of the energy requirements of large breeds, such as Boxers and German Shepherds in the 30–40 kg (66–88 lb) range.

Food types

By reading the labels on packets and cans, you can find out not only which ingredients are contained in commercial foods but also the percentage of proteins, carbohydrates, bulk vitamins and minerals. Most established manufacturers produce information

Feeding routines

Dog	Age	Number of meals	Type of meal
Active young adults	6–24 months	Two meals per day	Meat-based with biscuits or 'complete dried'; minimum protein content of 10% to maximum of 15%
Active adults	2–5 years	One/two meals per day	Meat-based with biscuits or 'complete dried'; minimum protein content of 10% to maximum of 15%
Adults	5 years +	One meal per day	Meat-based with biscuits or 'complete dried'; minimum protein content of 5% to maximum of 10%

Right: *Bland foods, such as scrambled egg, pasta and chicken, may be more suitable for elderly dogs or invalid dogs.*

guides on the correct quantities to be fed for different breeds, sizes and ages. There are a number of standard food types.

■ **Canned foods** contain processed ingredients and water in which essential vitamins and minerals can be lost.

■ **Premium dried foods** represent a balance between processed protein, vitamins and minerals, amino acids and bulk because they don't contain moisture and are more stable. Although it is convenient to store, it can be unappetizing to some dogs. Dried foods contain 'taste enhancers' to make them more attractive.

■ **Semi-moist foods and 'natural' meat foods** are similar to canned foods but are said to be appreciated by working dogs. **Note:** There are also basic meal biscuits or dry mixer biscuits which can be used to 'bulk' up canned foods.

Fresh foods

You can make up your own 'natural' dog food from fresh meat and rice or mixer biscuits. However, a meat and biscuit-only diet will not offer your dog the correct balance of protein, minerals, vitamins, fats, amino acids and bulk. Although natural food can be less frustrating than some commercial convenience foods, it should not be over-cooked; processed food speeds through the digestive system faster so blanching or part-cooking is better. You must mix meat and vegetables with mixer biscuits to ensure a dietary balance. Working breeds and aggressive dogs have been found by one researcher to be calmer when offered a natural diet.

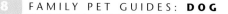

CHAPTER
FOUR

Left-overs

You can offer your dog left-overs from your meal provided they are added to his dish after you have finished eating. Most dogs enjoy a mixture of vegetables and meat scraps, thereby dispelling the myth that they are exclusively carnivores.

Treats, chews and bones

Dogs can be offered commercial dog treats and chews in addition to normal foods. These are best saved for training, walk and play times to promote obedient behaviour. Raw knuckle bones may be hard to acquire these days but dogs love to gnaw on them. Cooked bones can splinter (especially poultry, game and small meat pieces on the bone) and they should be avoided. A natural bone will keep a dog occupied for long periods although it is advisable to remove it at set periods to prevent possessive or obsessive behaviour and to establish your control. If your dog growls when you attempt to remove the bone, ignore the challenge, stand in another room and bounce a ball or rustle a bag. In most cases, your dog will leave the bone to investigate your actions. This 'distraction' method prevents 'confrontation' between you and your dog and reduces challenging behaviour. If you are using Training Discs (see page 87), they could be sounded to signal your dissatisfaction at his behaviour.

▎Walking and play

Most dogs will take as many walks as you offer. A healthy adult dog would benefit from two walks per day; one a lead-walking exercise and the other freestyle running with retrieve and recall games, provided that he responds obediently to commands.

All dogs need at least one daily walk, although elderly dogs tend to rest more and may require shorter ones than youngsters.

Play and walk times encourage a positive interaction with family and friends. Controlled walk and play sessions are best because they don't promote peaks of hyperactivity and exhaustion.

On walks, when your dog is off the lead, it is advisable to encourage random recall (see page 91). Use signal 'recall', with a whistle as well as a name call, especially if your dog is far away in the distance. Reward obedience with praise or a food treat. This interaction between you and your dog will promote obedience and keep his focus on you. When he has been trained to recall at your signal, you can attract him in situations of conflicting interest, such as strange dogs, livestock and people.

For young adults and older dogs, interactive play sessions with a retrieval ball or a thrown toy, at home and on walks, can be signalled with a 'reward whistle'. Restrict the sessions to short five-minute periods to prevent boisterousness and hyperactivity.

Games

You can encourage a positive relationship with your dog through play. Some aggressive behaviours can develop because of rough play. This is because play has its origins in pack-competition and hunting and killing in the wild.

■ **Tug-of-war games** are best avoided; they can encourage your dog to test his strength against yours. Competitive behaviour can lead to a dog confusing who is 'in charge of

Right: Walk your dog regularly from an early age, twice a day if possible for the more active breeds.

CHAPTER
FOUR

Right: *A food cube or ball will help prevent boredom.*

the pack'. Rubber rings, long pull-handled toys and 'raggers' among 'dominant' or status-seeking dogs can encourage aggression.

■ **Retrieval games**, where a ball or frisbee is thrown (retrieve with 'give' and recall instructions), are best for companion dogs. When your dog retrieves and gives up the item, he is being submissive. These games promote obedient behaviour.

■ **Hunting and foraging games** are fun and a great way to interact with your dog. Hide some food in the garden and then encourage him to find it. These games are ideal for working breeds, such as Retrievers, Springers, Pointers and Setters, which are not given the opportunity to work and perform the tasks for which they have been line-bred over generations.

In your absence, it is possible to relieve boredom and reduce distress with the use of interactive 'self-rewarding' foraging toys (balls or cubes that hold dried food). These should be casually introduced and removed to offer your dog some break from potential boredom if he is left alone for long periods. It is important for some dogs that you are not signalling your impending absence with a 'cue', such as a treat or a toy.

Left: *Most dogs enjoy playing retrieval games with a ball or a frisbee.*

▌Grooming

It is advisable to groom an adult dog, including short- and wire-haired breeds, on average two or three times per week. However, long-haired dogs may require daily grooming if their coats are to be properly maintained. If regular grooming sessions are promoted from early puppy days, it is unlikely that your dog will find them stressful and, indeed, they can be enjoyable for both of you.

Encourage your dog to 'stand' at each grooming session; if he lies down or proceeds to dance about during grooming, it is impossible to be thorough. In the case of boisterous dogs, it is advisable to offer a food treat reward when they stand and during grooming. Always have the brush ready in advance before calling your dog to be groomed. Regular attention to the coat will prevent matting and reduce natural hair loss in the home.

Grooming procedure

This will depend very much on your dog's coat. Short-haired dogs with a smooth coat will require only a quick brush to remove any dead hairs followed by a polish with a hound glove, chamois leather or cotton cloth. Long-haired breeds need extensive brushing and combing to remove dead hairs and tangles, and the grooming sessions will be more time-consuming.

Equipment

In order to groom your dog you will need the following:

- A soft brush
- A bristle brush
- A wide- or fine-toothed comb
- Some cotton cloth.

In addition, you may need a rubber slicker or hound glove, stripping comb, scissors and nail clippers, depending on the breed of dog and its coat type.

CHAPTER
FOUR

Grooming guidelines

1 Give your dog a quick brush to tease out any tangles and remove dead hairs. You may have to gently tease out any reluctant matted tangles with your fingers.

2 Gently comb through the coat, especially any long hair on the ears and tail feathering.

3 Follow up with a vigorous brushing.

4 You may wish to shine your dog's coat with a chamois leather or a damp cotton cloth to give it a healthy finish.

Note: Don't forget to brush around the anal area under the dog's tail and also its belly.

Above right: *Gently brush your dog's coat to remove any dead hairs.*

Left: *Carefully tease out any tangles in the long fur on your dog's head, ears, belly and tail.*

Right: *Your dog will probably enjoy all the attention as you brush him.*

Health check

While you are grooming your dog, take the opportunity to check for fleas, cuts and any signs of poor health.

1 Look carefully at his eyes, mouth and ears for any dirt or discharge. Always gently wipe these areas with a clean, damp cloth or cotton wool.

2 Check the claws and paw pads for potential damage. The claws can be trimmed with purpose-made clippers, but trimming should be slight and undertaken carefully to avoid cutting into the upper (pinkish) blood vessel region of each claw.

3 Check the teeth for any severe discolouring. You could incorporate cleaning the teeth with a special tooth brush and toothpaste into the grooming routine. This will help prevent tooth decay, gum disease and bad breath. Always consult your vet if you have any concerns for your dog's overall health.

Above: *After the grooming session, check your dog's eyes for signs of tear stains or any unusual discharge.*

Right: *Soft-mouthed dogs like Spaniels should have the folds of skin round their mouth regularly checked for food residues, which can cause bad breath or dental problems.*

CHAPTER
FOUR

▌Bathing your dog

You may need to bath or shower your dog occasionally, especially after a rain-soaked walk through muddy fields. Regular washing can become routine, especially if the ritual has been established

during the puppy period. Think of the procedure as a military-style operation with as little build-up as possible. Attach a short lead to your dog if he is likely to bound about during the washing.

Bathing guidelines

1 Fully soak your dog with lukewarm water, using a specially kept sponge or cloth. Be careful not to get any water inside his ears.

2 With a special dog shampoo or baby shampoo, lather the coat, taking care to avoid the eyes and ears. Do not be over-vigorous with the soaping as your dog needs to retain his natural oils to protect him from the cold and the wet.

3 Rinse out all the shampoo with lukwarm water, paying special attention to the legs, paws and rear.

4 Dry your dog thoroughly with an old towel which is kept specifically for this purpose (or use a hair dryer). Don't let him run around outside until he is thoroughly dry.

▍Bathing tips

- ■ Always use a specially formulated dog shampoo
- ■ Have the bath already partially filled with lukewarm water before you start
- ■ If you use a shower head, make sure the water is cool to touch.
- ■ Have several towels ready in anticipation of the inevitable water 'shake' behaviour following the bath or shower.

▌Car travel

Dogs and puppies should always be kept secure in vehicles for the safety of both driver and animal. Some hatchback cars and estates are easy to fit with 'dog fences' or bars to prevent movement in the passenger area of the car. Although your dog may prefer to sit on the front seat, any sudden braking could result in the dog being catapulted around the vehicle and injured. Car harnesses are also available to restrict a dog's movement and ensure that he is secure.

Travel crates or cages are ideal for car use and they are usually welcomed by your dog, provided they have been introduced at the puppy stage. Many people who show or breed dogs use travel crates because they know they provide a safety element in the event of a accident. Travel units are especially effective when covered, particularly for dogs that display car sickness, nervous, hyperactive or phobic behaviour, as visual triggers are reduced.

Below: *Travel cages can be fitted into the back of your car and will make transporting your dog(s) safer and easier.*

CHAPTER
FOUR

Holidays

You can take your dog on holiday provided that the hotel or accommodation confirms it is their policy to accept dogs. Travel crates are ideal for stays in hotels, cottages and caravans because a part of your dog's territory can go with him. You can also be confident that he cannot bolt and then become lost and disorientated in an unfamiliar environment.

Dog sitters and friends

Many owners ask a family member or friend to act as 'dog sitter' while they are away as dogs prefer to stay in their own home where they feel secure. However, your dog could stay at a friend's home or you could arrange a sitter from an agency. Or your dog can even live in a 'family home' where people offer a short-term personal dog-sitting service.

Boarding kennels

These are best recommended by a friend or your vet. Make an appointment to visit and inspect prospective kennels. Some owners use the kennels initially for just one day or a weekend to ensure their pet is not adversely affected. All reputable kennels need to see a veterinary vaccination certificate confirming that your dog is protected against Weils disease, parvovirus, canine hepatitis and kennel cough. Even if your dog has been vaccinated, he may benefit from a booster. If you aren't sure whether he is up-to-date with vaccinations, consult your vet.

Taking your dog abroad

It is now possible to take your dog abroad, provided that a dog passport has been obtained. However, the procedures require micro-chipping your dog and arranging a rabies vaccination followed by, 30 days later, a blood test. Even then, your dog cannot go abroad for six months. Your vet may have an information leaflet giving details of a government help-line and website.

Adopting a 'rescue or re-homed' dog

When you first collect a rescue or re-homed dog, it is important to consider what the journey represents from a 'confused canine' viewpoint. The dog won't know you nor where he is being taken or for how long. All the journey represents is the 'unknown' and therefore a potentially frightening new phase in his life.

A covered travel or folding crate, containing an attached water bottle, is probably the best way for the dog to travel. He doesn't need cradling on someone's knee and won't appreciate the 'competing attention' of young children. It is advisable that only one adult collects the dog to keep any fuss to a minimum.

Arriving home

When you arrive home, transfer the crate to a designated area within your house and give the dog an hour or so to take in the strange smells of his new home. After some settling-in time, open the door of the crate and let him decide when to come out. One or two people could be seated close by to reassure him. Some dogs will bound out like a playful puppy whereas others will be introverted and hesitate to leave the comfort of their confined space. It is important not to humanize the situation. Travel or folding crates, which are covered and bottom layered with a blanket, represent a bolt hole or burrow and, as such, offer the dog a secure place in a time of confusion.

Right: *After he has explored his new home, a quiet grooming session may help to settle your new pet. Never force him as that can damage your relationship.*

CHAPTER
FOUR

Settling in

The next stage is to allow the dog to explore your immediate garden, provided that this area is properly fenced and there is no chance of escape. The first few days of a rescued dog's re-homed life will be over-shadowed with confusion, and the last thing you want is for the dog to escape into the unknown. To speed up the acceptance of his new territory, the transfer of soiled newspaper, bedding material or faeces will encourage an insecure dog to mark or scent again outside. The chosen item can be placed in a suitable area of the garden. The rescue organisation may look at you with disbelief when you request soiled items but your answer could be to quote this section!

Food and water

Feeding the dog should not be considered a priority. Although some dogs will 'wolf down' the first food offered as though they are famished, there is good reason to give low priority to feeding.

The dog's first night can be filled with confusion because of the strangeness of the surroundings – in stark contrast to life in the shelter or kennels – and the newness of the people around him. Any stress coupled with a potential change in diet could cause the onset of extremely 'loose' bodily functions during the night, and the scene that may greet your family in the morning could be daunting.

Left: *Let your new friend explore the garden, which will be full of fascinating new smells. Give him time to familiarize himself.*

Above: *When settling a rescue dog into his new home, tell him to sit and offer him a biscuit or treat to calm him down.*

Although it is vital to provide a permanent source of clean water, there is no need to offer a similar bowl of food. If your dog appears willing to settle immediately, it is reasonable to offer a few dry dog biscuits in a controlled situation. Tell the dog to sit and offer him a biscuit or two. All members of the family could join in this exercise provided that the dog is not hyperactive and that the type of food is not high in protein or offered in excess.

Health check

It would be advisable to get him examined by your vet to confirm a 'clean bill of health'; have him inoculated if necessary. Make an appointment to take him along in the first few days.

CHAPTER
FOUR

The effects of a change of home

It is important to consider that a rescue dog may have experienced multiple ownership and this aspect could influence his behaviour. There will undoubtedly have been inconsistencies in handling, which could include control, diet, housing, bedding, toileting, periods left at 'home alone', and human and canine family size.

Always start from the position that the dog may have suffered the worst and expect, if a canine can be described as such, a cynical animal. Your consistency will shine through before any other attribute you may have to share with your new chum.

The unpredictability of an 'unknown past' can present a challenge to the conscientious 'rescue dog' owner. The potential for difficulties should not deter you if you are determined to help out a canine in care. It would be an extremely disturbed dog that did not respond to handling consistency, especially when this is directed into the right care and attention.

The first night

Use the travel crate for at least the first night and offer the dog an opportunity to toilet before settling him down. The first meal, following diet suggestions from the rescue organisation, should be offered the following day after he has been lead-exercised and allowed to settle into his new home. He may refuse the food initially; if so, pick up the dish and put it down again later or the following day. Your dog will not starve if, in the early settling-down period, he chooses to fast for a few days.

Introductions to existing pets

Some rescue dogs are brought home to a family that already has pets. Ask the staff at the rescue if they know whether your new friend has been socialized with other dogs or cats. If they don't know, any early contact must be in a controlled situation.

It is vital that any early encounters with other dogs occur on neutral ground and that the new dog is not introduced to an existing dog within the confines of the home. If there are no signs of aggression, then the introduction to home can be achieved rapidly. Any challenge from either animal immediately makes integration a much more gradual process.

You can use travel crates to initially confine two 'un-socialized' dogs. One can be let out and given the 'run' of the available space within the home and garden. Then the other can be given the same freedom. Ideally, the two dogs should be introduced on neutral territory. Eventually both could be released together at home and shown a reward, either your physical attention or treats, for appropriate behaviour. Training discs (see page 88) can be used immediately to develop an association between a sound and non-reward for any unwanted aggressive behaviour.

Dogs and cats

If your new dog has not been previously socialized with cats and you own one, early introductions must be controlled and the cat should be given the opportunity to escape unwanted attention. If the dog chases after your cat, recall him quickly and reward him on his

Right: *Most dogs, if introduced correctly and early enough, show no aggression towards what would be their natural prey. But never allow your dog to have unsupervised access to a small pet.*

return. Puppies usually adapt to cats and vice versa. Most of the attention on both sides is based on natural curiosity and play. Some dogs may have been encouraged to chase cats, and it may take some repetitive training to change or counter-condition this. Cats often get the better of dogs, and long-term problems are unlikely in all but the most aggressive animals.

Young children

Introducing the new rescue dog to young children should also be carefully planned. Some dogs are nervous of small humans: they may have been tormented by children or may never have been

Above: *Children love playing with dogs but make sure that they are supervised for both their sakes, as dogs can behave nervously and young children can be very unpredictable.*

Rescue at hand

If rescue dogs are humanized, a distressed and confused animal's psychological problems will be encouraged or reinforced. Thus it is vital that a rescued dog is treated firmly and consistently. The first few weeks in a new home are the most important when it comes to establishing a secure territory and a healthy owner-pet relationship. Dogs do not wander around stroking and patting each other. This is for our benefit, not the dog's. Stroking a dog can be a stress buster, lowering our blood pressure and reducing heart rate, and, for a secure dog, a continuous supply of pats and strokes can become established in a stable relationship as 'normal' behaviour. It's what the master wants! To an insecure and disorientated dog, excessive stroking and patting can be perceived as a signal of confusion and will only feed its insecurity.

It is admirable that people should want to make up for the difficult life that a rescued dog may have suffered. However, such kindness should be channelled through company, good food, warm bedding and plenty of controlled walks. Coupled with firm and consistent control, all dogs offered food and a home will respond to their owners in a positive way.

exposed to them in their previous home. Young children can be very unpredictable with regards to certain sounds and movements, which is disturbing for a nervous dog with a difficult background.

The best moment to introduce children to a new dog is during play. The play period should be short and interesting and held in a secure, open area or where the dog can be contained, such as a garden or enclosed field. A ball game of retrieval and reward is a good way to develop a controlled interrelationship between dogs and young children. Lots of food rewards for recall, sit and offering up the ball will usually cement the start of a good relationship between a nervous dog and children.

CHAPTER FIVE

Training your dog

A well-behaved dog is a joy to own and a credit to you, and that is why it is so important that you train your pet to respond to simple commands.

Training is not an unpleasant chore; indeed, it can be fun for both of you and will bring many benefits. A well-trained dog can be exercised safely in public places, socialize with other dogs, be trusted with adults and children, and can be an accepted member of your family and society.

It is very satisfying to keep a well-behaved dog, but the first steps to training your pet often require unlimited patience and understanding. However, the rewards, such as when your dog learns a new command, can be rewarding for both of you and make all the hard work worthwhile.

▍Training begins at home

Some of the most beneficial 'training' can be gained from 'throw and fetch' games in your home or garden. They are enjoyable for your dog and can also be fun for you. With some effort and patience, you can quickly

CHAPTER
FIVE

Training guidelines

1 Make training sessions fun for both of you.
2 Be patient and be prepared to progress gradually.
3 Keep the training sessions short to prevent boredom setting in.
4 Reward good behaviour with praise and treats.
5 Never shout at your dog or punish him.
6 Teach one thing at a time – don't introduce too many commands at once.
7 Always use the same command words – and make sure your family does, too.

teach your dog to chase and retrieve a ball or toy bone, recall, give and then sit for a reward. The reward can be either a pat, a vocal congratulation and a treat or, initially, a combination of all three. Some dogs respond better to these games than others.

It is possible, with a food reward, to encourage your pet to 'give' you the toy it has brought back to you. This game includes many important 'control' factors and will encourage 'submissive' obedience.

Teach with enthusiasm

Try not to become frustrated if your puppy appears to ignore some of your efforts to train him. A puppy can sense your feelings and will often exploit any situation he can turn into a game.

■ If he refuses to 'come' on your instruction, use distraction to obtain his attention – for instance, sound a whistle, a novel squeaky toy or rustle a treat package. He will soon come running if he thinks you have something he might want.

■ Do not scold your puppy if he returns late to your signal as this will promote mistrust. Always praise your dog enthusiastically for his eventual obedience. If recall is a real problem, use an extending lead or line to create control at a distance.

■ It is vital that you do not smack your dog or shout at him aggressively. These actions will encourage mistrust and even aggression or nervousness in dogs. Shouting at your puppy is 'barking' according to a dog's hearing sensitivity.

■ Always signal problem behaviour with a sharp, low-toned 'No' or with training discs (see page 86). However, good behaviour can always be promoted with a food reward and vocal and physical praise.

Training rewards

Always praise your dog for responding to your training instructions. Nearly all dogs respond well to food rewards and these can be used to good effect in training. Keep some titbits in your pocket or hand during training sessions to reward good behaviour. Use the specially formulated dried food treats and dog biscuits, which are available from most pet stores and general supermarkets, or liver treats (see page 78). However, in difficult or acute conditions and in the long-term rehabilitation

Above and right: *Always reward your dog with a titbit or praise when he is obedient and responds to your commands. Reward-based training is always the most effective.*

CHAPTER
FIVE

Liver treats

450 g/1 lb chopped pig's or lamb's liver
450 g/1 lb plain flour
2 eggs
1 teaspoon garlic powder
water, to moisten

Place all the ingredients in a food processor and blend together. Spread out the blended mixture on a baking tray and cook in a preheated oven at 180°C/350°F/Gas 4 for 30–40 minutes, or until cooked through and firm. Cool and cut into small squares. Store in a sealed container in the refrigerator.

Note: Liver treats should be used sparingly and in small amounts.

of dogs with behavioural problems, it can be important to experiment with different types of food rewards.

When a 'reward whistle' is being established (see page 87), or when you are teaching 'recall', interrupting hyperactivity towards strangers and other dogs, initiating short retrieval sessions or retrieval of a personal item, such as a shoe or clothing, it is advisable to use a 'significant' food reward, such as meat or dried liver.

However, you can also experiment with other types of reward, such as an enthusiastic pat and praise, a novel toy or a squeaky ball. Some dog trainers have found that different rewards work in different situations.

▌ Teaching the basic commands

Start off by teaching your puppy the basic command words, which should be accompanied by obvious hand signals. These might include the following:

■ **'Come'**: wave your hand towards you or pat your knee.

■ **'Sit'**: hold your hand out with your palm facing down in front of your puppy.
■ **'Down'**: point down to the floor and draw your puppy down from the sit position.
■ **'Move off'**: keep your hand pointing forwards.
■ **'Walk to heel'**: keep your hand by your side.

It is not the 'words' that the puppy begins to understand but the 'sounds' and the actions, events or hand signals that are immediately linked to them. For example, if you announce the word 'walkies' to your puppy and then attach a lead to his collar, a powerful association with the sound 'K' will be made with the promise of a walk.

After about three or four months, your puppy should understand most of the basic commands and will enjoy responding to them. Older dogs that have been untrained may take longer to accept new signals.

Remember that your puppy will always learn best when he is enjoying himself. For this reason, daily training sessions should be short and enjoyable. Try not to become 'angry' or disappointed with your puppy should he fail to respond to your commands as it can take a number of attempts to successfully accomplish a new instruction. Always reward your puppy with praise and a stroke when he responds well.

Right: *You can teach an old dog new tricks but it may take a lot longer and need constant reinforcing.*

CHAPTER
FIVE

Come

The first instruction word to teach is 'come'. You can begin teaching your puppy to 'come' to your command in the home when he is very young. Using a cheerful tone of voice, always address your puppy by his name. He will quickly learn his name and then you can begin simple training instructions. Dogs learn by association, actions or events.

In the house or garden, you should instruct your puppy to 'come' after calling out his name in a confident tone of voice. In the early days of training you can also use gestures, such as patting your knee, to visually encourage your pet to recall to your instruction. If you praise and reward him when he responds, he will associate 'recall' with his name and the word 'come' together with a happy moment – your stroking and praise.

1 Walk away from your dog and then call him to you, using his name and the word 'come'.

2 As he runs towards you, hold out a treat and praise him enthusiastically.

Training tip

It is important not to make any act of 'aggression' or disobedience exciting by offering your dog excessive attention as this will only turn the event into a 'game' and will encourage problem behaviours. Always finish a session on a positive note with a 'well-rewarded' 'click and treat' control walk or a brief retrieval session with a ball.

Sit

When your puppy responds to his name and the 'come' command, you can teach him to sit. Some people teach the 'sit' command by gently but firmly pushing the dog's bottom down, but do not use too much force. An alternative teaching method is shown below.

1 Holding a food reward above your puppy's head, tell him in a low-toned voice to 'Sit'. He should be looking up at the food.
2 As he looks up, move the food over his head and as he continues looking up at it, his back legs should go down naturally into the 'sit' position. Give him the reward and praise him.

CHAPTER
FIVE

Down

Teaching the 'down' command is a natural progression from 'sit'. Don't be frustrated if your dog almost makes the 'down' position but rises up at the last minute. Repeated attempts, with food rewards as a reinforcement, will eventually ensure success. If he stays in the down position, step back in an attempt to put some distance, however slight, between you. This will lead you perfectly onto the next step in training which involves 'stay'.

1 Using a food reward as a lure, draw your dog's head down towards the ground from a 'sit' position.

2 Lower the treat to the ground just in front of his nose, drawing it along the ground towards you.

3 Your dog will stretch out his front legs and lower himself into the down position. Praise him and repeat the word 'down' several times so he associates the sound of the word with his position.

Stay

Teaching a dog the 'stay' command requires plenty of patience and kindness. Once you have mastered 'down' encouraging your dog to stay in place is a natural progression.

1 Instruct your dog to go 'down' or 'sit' and then slowly back away from him.

2 Move a few paces away from the dog, holding out your hand and repeating 'Stay'. Keep eye contact throughout.

3 As soon as your dog makes the first body language signs that he will move towards you, call him to you. Once your dog returns to you praise him and reward with a food treat. Over several sessions build the time up he 'stays' until he 'stays' with only a single word command. Clicker training is excellent for this stage.

CHAPTER
FIVE

Lead-walking

When your puppy is about twelve weeks old, you can start teaching him how to walk to your heel on a lead. Before you start formal training, you will have to get him used to wearing a collar and lead. You could attach a lead to his collar for short periods and let him run around the house or garden like this. He will soon get accustomed to it. Outside of your home or garden, it is essential to keep him on a close lead – not too ong and keeping him close beside you. This will 'transmit' your control and confidence and will prevent your puppy leaping about becoming distracted.

While walking, keep your puppy close to your side. If he pulls, stop and instruct him to walk to 'heel' in a firm, clear voice,

drawing him nearer to your side. When he responds, give the 'sit' command and only continue walking when he has obeyed. This will signal to him that pulling is unacceptable and that he has to accept your control.

1 With the puppy on your right side, hold the lead in your left hand. Use a food reward to encourage him to move forwards and walk at your side.
2 Say 'Heel' firmly and start walking, keeping him close to your side with the lead slightly slack.
3 If the puppy pulls forwards and the lead becomes taut, stop him and tell him to 'Sit' at your side.
4 When he sits down, say 'Heel' and start walking again.

CHAPTER
FIVE

▌ 'Psychological training' with aids

Once your puppy has progressed with training and becomes more confident and adventurous outdoors, it may be necessary to use training aids to reinforce obedient behaviour. Adopted and rescue dogs invariably need incentives to respond to their new owners.

Clicker signalling

One successful training method is to use 'positive reinforcement' (using rewards to promote good behaviour) through clicker signalling. A 'clicker' is a thumb-sized plastic unit with a thin metal film which, when pressed, sends out a double click sound when depressed. The principle to be applied, based on 'classical conditioning', is that this unique sound, when linked to a food reward, will signal to your dog that a treat is about to be given. This 'promise' of reward, when used as your puppy or dog correctly responds to training, will promote obedience.

The clicker is only sounded when your pet has responded to instructions, such as 'Sit', 'Stay' and 'Come'. Eventually, the sound, which is not voice or tone dependent so as to enable everyone in the family to use this form of reinforcement, will become embedded in your pet's subconscious and then can be used to promote all kinds of good behaviour. For example, the clicker should be used when greeting your dog once he has responded to your 'Sit' instruction.

It may take a few attempts to 'condition' your dog to associate the sound of the clicker with the 'reward'. However,

❖ Clicker

❖ Training discs

❖ Reward whistle

Above: *When you are out walking your dog, you can use the clicker to reinforce his good behaviour when he responds correctly to your commands.*

once he understands that the clicker is a signal for 'reward', he will respond without too much encouragement. Initially the reward should be food-based – dog biscuits or small pieces of meat – but eventually it can be a pat or some words of praise.

Reward whistle

A 'reward whistle', when linked to a significant food reward and accepted by your dog, can be used like a clicker to promote recall at a distance on walks or at home. Some dogs have 'selective hearing' insofar as they prefer to follow a scent or chase

CHAPTER
FIVE

after other dogs rather than return to your side when instructed.

It is important that the chosen sound-signals are linked to a 'reward' to motivate your dog to respond. It is also vital that the sound-signals are used randomly during the initial exposure so that he does not 'associate' the whistle with a particular event, such as the arrival of a family member, visitor, another dog or the postman.

All good behaviour should be signalled with a 'click' and reinforced with an appropriate dog 'treat' – not chocolate or cheese because these foods may encourage hyperactivity and can be detrimental to your dog's health.

Disc training

Training discs are the opposite of a reward signal. They are used to signal that you wish a particular behaviour to cease – through negative reinforcement, i.e. the removal of reward. The use of training discs, together with the removal/denial of reward, will teach your dog to stop displaying an unwanted behaviour. They are especially useful for rescue, re-homed and older dogs that have not been trained.

The use of discs started with the idea that a simple, easy-to-make sound could signal to a dog that a particular behaviour, such as jumping up or growling, should cease. The five 5-cm (2-in) sized brass discs are held together on a handy cord. When they are shaken and dangled or dropped on to the ground, they make a very distinctive sound.

Once your puppy or dog has been conditioned to understand that the sound of the discs represent the 'removal of a reward' (the opposite to the clicker) they can be used to deal with many problem behaviours, such as rushing through doors, excessive barking and forms of attention seeking.

The discs are not meant to scare your puppy or dog. They signal that a particular behaviour is not wanted. Always hold on to them if there is a possibility that your dog may pick them up.

Introducing the discs

The first steps to teaching and 'conditioning' your puppy or dog to the training discs will require a brief session in which they are introduced. Follow these simple guidelines:

1 Call your dog to you, tell him to 'Sit' and then offer him a treat from your hand.

2 Place a treat on the ground between your feet (with small- to medium-sized dogs, this is best accomplished when you are seated) and then move your hand away.

3 As your dog attempts to take the treat, quickly put it in your pocket and put down the discs instead. You need not throw the discs or rattle them excessively – they only need to make a sound. You then repeat the exercise by replacing the food treat between your feet and then removing it again when your dog goes to take it. Eventually, your dog will sit down or withdraw.

Note: This is the first step to teaching your dog or puppy, subconsciously, that the training discs mean non-reward and a particular behaviour isn't wanted.

CHAPTER
FIVE

Training or 'controlled' walks

When the basic commands have been learned, it should be possible to continue training exercises whilst out on walks. It is important to have complete control of your dog when he is in a public place, and he should only be allowed to run freely off the lead when you are confident that 'recall' is 100 per cent successful. As your healthy puppy grows, he will become stronger, and with medium to large breeds it is essential that control is maintained. For this reason, it is important to play the role of 'pack leader' on short training walks. Showing that you are 'in charge' is not about physically restraining your dog; it is better that you offer psychological restraint in an intensive training session to promote control.

1 Walk your dog or puppy on a short lead to keep him at your side – do not use a 'choke' check-chain. The 'Halti' or 'Gentle Leader' aids are ideal for preventing a dog pulling.

Right: *A Gentle Leader head collar will give you total control over your dog and prevent him pulling or lungeing.*

Recall problems

You must work on repeated, random recalls (at home and on walks) with your dog. If he refuses to obey a recall, supervise his behaviour with a 'lunge line' or an extending lead, together with a 'Halti' or 'Gentle Leader' and, possibly, a muzzle during long walks where he may encounter strangers and display aggression. This level of supervision can be reduced when he has 'learned' new routines and has improved recall during walks.

2 Choose a number of roadside landmarks near your home, such as lamp posts and gateways, and halt your dog at each. In a low voice, say 'Sit', then 'click', 'reward' and praise his behaviour.
3 Tell him to move on when you're ready – say 'Go' or 'Walk on' or 'OK'. If he pulls, tell him quietly to 'Sit' – don't shout at him.
Note: Click and treat each instruction that has been obeyed to promote good behaviour. Don't move on to the next instruction until your dog has responded obediently. If he then ignores you, let him smell a treat but do not offer it to him until the instruction is obeyed.

Well-trained walks

Walks represent 'hunting and foraging' episodes to dogs. This is why they become excited by the prospect of a walk and respond immediately to visual and sound behavioural cues – changing shoes, putting on a coat or picking up keys. Try to reduce these stimuli and make less 'fuss' prior to walks.

Some nervous dogs can be stubborn about walks, even refusing them, because they cannot 'control' these events. It is

CHAPTER
FIVE

normal behaviour for your dog to explore and become excited during walks. General walks can become more controlled if you observe the following guidelines.

1 At home, during a short session in the garden, sound a 'reward whistle', recall your dog and offer a click/food reward for sitting by your side. Repeat this five or six times.

2 Once it has proved successful, you can follow this sequence with the retrieval of favourite toy, such as a frisbee or ball, and further success should prove beneficial for training during freestyle walks.

3 Phase out the food reward over the weeks and replace some with some words of praise and a pat.

If you experience problems on walks, the random use of the 'reward whistle' is essential. If your dog is only recalled during 'exciting events' (encounters with dogs and strangers) he will make an association. 'Freestyle' walks can still be enjoyed but you must exercise control. During early retraining, it may be better to prevent him meeting strangers and use an extending lead.

A new route will encourage your dog to be more responsive to signals. Try distraction if he exhibits aggressive or excitable behaviour: tail out, hair standing up, lunging, pulling, barking or growling. Sound a whistle or a squeaky toy, call him to your side and tell him to 'Sit'. Immediately offer him a 'click' and a significant food reward, such as some cooked liver or chicken. If he is not 'treat' orientated, use a novel toy to hold his attention.

▌Controlled play

Play is an important part of a dog's day. You must always be 'in charge' and create several 'controlled' five-minute play periods. Don't allow your pet to become possessive over toys. When you wish to remove them after a play session, use distraction (e.g. a whistle) to call your dog to you and pat him for being obedient, or 'click and treat' to recall him and tell him to 'Sit'.

When toys are not being played with, put them away. Reward submissive behaviour when he 'fetches' or 'gives' you a toy with a food treat, a pat or praise. When a toy has been retrieved, tell your dog to 'Sit' and make him give up the toy immediately.

Tug-of-war games with pull or rag toys should not be used as they can encourage your pet to test his strength against yours. Outdoor games, which should last no longer than five to ten minutes, can be developed with a ball or frisbee. Your dog should be encouraged to retrieve a toy and then be patted or 'clicked and treated' for offering it up. It is important that the game is ceased on your instruction ('game over') with the object in your possession and that the toy is replaced in the toy box.

Right: *Your puppy or dog should soon learn to understand and obey simple commands. Note that this Labrador puppy has not been rewarded until he has calmly sat down after retrieving a toy. You can reward good behaviour with a treat and praise.*

CHAPTER SIX

Behavioural problems

A properly socialized puppy will rarely show problem behaviours. However, dogs that have not had the benefit of such socialization and rescue or re-homed dogs may show 'unpredictable behaviour' in the first few months of being introduced into a new family.

Antisocial, unpredictable or problem behaviour can sometimes be nothing more than 'testing' behaviour where a dog refuses to respond to an instruction or growls over food. In more serious conditions, aggression, excessive barking, destructiveness, toileting in the home and withdrawn behaviour may be displayed. Sometimes incorrect handling can trigger a dog to adopt an instinctive 'round up and nip' or 'bite and control' mode of behaviour.

Even dogs who have experienced normal socialization from the puppy stage can be triggered into nervous responses. These triggers can be unavoidable, such as house moves or a change in a relationship, but consistent handling will usually smooth out any temporary problems.

Thankfully, most problem behaviours can be dealt with by a correct response from the dog's owner, and the increased use of clicker and disc communication (see pages 86 and 88) to signal 'good or bad' behaviour to the dog.

CHAPTER
SIX

PROBLEM BEHAVIOUR

Some problem behaviours can be changed simply by re-training. Other antisocial forms of behaviour, however, are more acute and will need more radical treatment to cure them.

▌Jumping up

Jumping up can usually be prevented by re-training the dog, especially if he jumps up at members of your family, friends or visitors. It is possible that this undesirable behaviour has been promoted in the past because some people enjoy a boisterous greeting from their dog.

In this instance, the first step is to embark on a programme of ignoring your dog on entry. Ask people to play the role of visitors and to ignore your dog until he has quietened down. Any undue attention that is given to a boisterous dog will only promote hyperactivity. Once your dog begins to quieten down, it is possible to move on to the second stage, which is to offer the dog a pat or a stroke or even to 'click and treat' (see page 86) to reinforce his 'good behaviour'.

▌Nervous behaviour

Some dogs can become very attached to their owners, following them around and continually seeking attention. It would be easy to think of this as 'bonding', but this is not usual behaviour for happy dogs. Sometimes dogs that make a strong attachment become emotionally disturbed when left in the home alone.

■ Dogs that display 'disturbed behaviours' in the home, such as destructiveness (chewing, scratching and digging), excessive barking/howling/whining or inappropriate urination and/or defecation in your absence, are generally suffering from insecurity; the condition is known as Separation-Related-Disorder (SRD). These dogs are often 'over-dependent' on individuals within the family.

■ Dogs that display hyperactivity when travelling in vehicles are showing 'association' distress, are over-stimulated, hyper-alert or have suffered negative associations with a journey.

■ Dogs that suffer from 'over-alertness' or show 'fear or territorial aggression' towards people or dogs are also insecure.

These conditions may vary from moderate to acute, with some animals displaying extreme neurotic responses. Most 'antisocial behaviours' represent an outlet for a dog's emotional 'separation' distress, and/or its reaction to boredom and 'faulty

Above: *Although some dogs enjoy car travel, others display hyperactive behaviour and become distressed in vehicles, possibly due to negative associations with cars.*

**CHAPTER
SIX**

learning', which develops during the litter and early juvenile periods. Dogs that have suffered shifts in territory (rescue and re-homed animals) or have moved between locations often suffer from separation-related disorders, over-alertness and hyperactivity.

Treating general insecurity

A general calming programme will help to treat any general insecurity in your dog. The next stage is to randomly leave him alone in the house, but returning almost immediately and praising calm behaviour. The period of separation should be increased gradually over time. Avoid any interaction with him for 15–20 minutes before you leave and greet him with an instruction to 'Sit'. Offer a reward (click and treat, praise or a pat) on your return as this unemotional strategy will help reduce the contrast between your presence and absence and will diminish excitability.

You can also use travel crates, covered at the top and base-lined with a favourite blanket, to confine your dog overnight or for limited 'random' periods while the family is at home. The security offered by a 'crate', which represents a den to your dog, will often eliminate distress-related problems, such as destructive

Right: *A crate will be perceived as a secure, safe den by a dog, and can help treat behaviour problems.*

Guidelines for using a crate

1 The crate should be just large enough for your dog to stand up in – not too large as it is not intended to be an exercise unit but a place where the dog can rest.

2 Preferably, the crate should be collapsible and fit within your car. Cover the crate to create a 'den' effect.

3 The crate should not be used for visits to the vet or for punishment to avoid potential negative associations. It should be used if you move house, travel, stay in a caravan or boat, or when taking your dog on visits to other people's homes.

4 Place the dog's bedding inside and leave the door open. If he ignores the crate, place an enticing toy inside and give him time and privacy to discover his new 'den'. The best is at night when the dog would be relaxing naturally and is ready to rest.

5 It is a good idea to put an item of your old clothing inside the crate (re-scent the item by wearing it or by leaving it in a washing basket for a day) to encourage your dog to explore the unit. Random crating is best to avoid any 'association'.

6 If your dog shows little sign of entering the crate (after several daytime and overnight periods), you must be firm and order him to enter. Back him into the crate and close the door. Leave him alone for about 5–10 minutes, then return. Open the door, praise him and let him exit of his own accord. Repeat several times during the day and for the last period at night.

behaviour and inappropriate urination or defecation. It can help make him feel more secure and prevent inappropriate behaviour until a calming programme begins to take effect.

To treat SRD effectively, encourage your dog to spend short periods of time alone in the garden, his bed, crate or a separate room, but not when visitors arrive because the isolation will have a negative association. Instead, isolate the dog prior to their

CHAPTER
SIX

arrival. Ask your guests not to 'fuss' over the dog; this will reduce excitability. A pat and a treat in reward for sitting are sufficient.

To make your absence less marked, especially in cases of noise phobia, leave a 'talk' radio programme playing and provide a durable chew or ball to help reduce potential boredom. In acute cases of SRD, consult your vet who will probably refer you and your pet to an animal behaviour therapist.

▌ Obsessive barking

Excessive barking, especially from a hyperactive dog, is usually linked to 'attention seeking' or 'fear and territorial aggression'. Barking can be promoted (often when dogs are puppies) if owners 'bark' back by shouting. Dogs have sensitive hearing,

Dealing with separation

In the first stage of dealing with owner-absence SRD problems, you should provide chews, meat bones or an interactive, self-rewarding toy, such as a foraging ball or a 'Buster Cube', as these can offer a 'displacement reward' during periods of isolation when separation distress – excessive barking, destructiveness and inappropriate urination – is shown. These 'activity' items should be put down discretely during the period before you leave the house and should be removed after you return in order to maintain their novelty value.

Above: *Leave a radio on and give your dog a food ball or some chews and toys when you leave him alone in the house.*

and the result of shouting can be a 'barking competition' between the owner and dog.

In dogs suffering from a nervous condition, unusual sounds, strangers and other dogs are perceived as a threat. Barking is not only a way of warning the 'pack' but is also meant to warn away the threat. Happy and healthy dogs only bark briefly and do not vocalize excessively at everyday events.

CHAPTER
SIX

▍ **Why aggression?**

Aggressive behaviour is rewarded in one of the following ways:
■ An advantage in sex, food or territory is gained
■ Something feared is 'driven away' or escaped from after which the animal is rewarded by relief.

The intensity of 'relief' gained by some dogs, i.e. success in chasing off a perceived threat, such as a dog or postman, is often greater than any 'benefit' gained from the aggressive action. This aspect can develop addictive behaviour (associated stimuli) if the frequency of aggression increases and is self-reinforcing.

Many aspects of dog aggression are linked to fear. House moves and frequent visitors can trigger behavioural problems. Some dogs perceive other dogs or strangers as a threat to their 'human-canine pack and home territory. People and dogs usually leave the scene following the bout of aggressive behaviour (going about their daily business), and this helps to reinforce the dog's idea that he has succeeded in 'chasing off' a perceived threat.

Aggressive behaviours

There are many types of aggression that are recognised in dogs:
■ Intraspecific – dog versus dog
■ Predatory – attack and bite
■ Possessive – growling and refusing to give up items
■ Protective – warning off or attacking a perceived threat
■ Fear and territorial – reacting in a fight or flight response to a feared target or when protecting its home and property.

These are exhibited in various degrees, depending on whether the nervous condition is mild or acute. They range from hyperactivity to antisocial behaviour. Most forms of aggression are directed towards other dogs and/or owners and strangers. A 'nervous' dog will growl at, bark, lunge, snap, nip at or chase a target it considers threatening. These behaviours are 'instinctive' but can also be 'learned' in the early stages of development or when the dog has been attacked by another dog. The fear of attack can promote a 'get in first' behaviour which is linked to fear. Aggression based on fear can be inadvertently encouraged by inconsistent or passive owner control and suggests 'insecurity' in dogs. Happy dogs do not display aggression.

Dominant or status-seeking' behaviour and related challenging and aggressive behaviours can be exhibited if a dog is unsure of its place with the people within its 'perceived pack' (the family). It may have an inherited dominant trait and/or have experienced poor socialization. Often it may perceive itself in a 'leader role' (alpha) within the family and may believe certain areas and items, such as its bed, toys or the garden, are its territory or possessions. A dominant dog may also see family members as subdominant within the human-canine pack.

A dominant dog displaying aggression may attempt to 'control' or protect family individuals as it believes its role is to control and protect the 'pack'. Sometimes aggressive behaviour is also linked to 'challenging' and may be associated with food, or when a target is perceived as threatening. A nervous dog may display

Right: *You should be in total control at feeding time and should be able to remove your dog's food without him showing any aggression even if he hasn't finished eating.*

CHAPTER
SIX

Rewards

In difficult or acute behavioural problems, it may be useful to experiment with different types of food rewards. Daily training, including controlled walks and controlled play, can be rewarded with standard dog treats or biscuits. In more complex training, e.g. when the 'reward whistle' is being established, try a more 'significant' food reward, such as some meat or dried liver. Different rewards work in different situations.

aggression if people appear frightened or submissive. Such dogs often show persistent 'disobedience' with their owners such as refusing to recall (selective hearing) or sit on command.

In rehabilitating a dog displaying excessive aggression, you must reduce any patrolling or guarding behaviour. Interrupt all territorial aggression (growling, barking or lunging) with the reward whistle system or training discs (see page 88). Restrict any vantage points, such as an armchair at the window or a window ledge. If the hallway is a central point of aggression, make that area unavailable by closing doors or using a barrier. Restrict upper room and garden access to reduce 'patrolling' behaviour.

You can unintentionally 'reward' excessive guarding behaviour by shouting. Instead, use the clicker and disc system (see pages 86 and 88) to change the behaviour: click and treat good behaviour and signal 'non-reward' with the discs for inappropriate behaviour.

It is a good idea to pay less attention to the dog and stroke and pet him less than usual, to offer 'calming' signs. Dogs don't go around stroking or fussing each other and so they will often respond to a calmer approach to their relationship with owners.

TREATING PROBLEM BEHAVIOUR

Creating 'controlled' scenarios

This is a treatment for excessive barking, excitability, nervousness or aggression towards visitors, strangers and children in the home or on walks. Once the 'calming' method starts taking effect, try to change your dog's behaviour to strangers. Set up a 'controlled' scenario with a friend and/or child who is/are not fearful of dogs.

Step 1

■ Choose a neutral area, such as a field or neighbour's garden. The person or child/children should approach from the side.

■ As they do so, tell your dog to 'Sit' and reward his obedience with a treat or a pat. Click and treat the good behaviour.

■ If your dog looks or barks at the person, attract his attention with a squeaky toy or whistle, then tell him to 'Sit' and reward him. Any signs of nervous aggression should be signalled with

CHAPTER
SIX

the training discs; the session should be momentarily suspended.

■ If your dog is under control (showing little or no excitability to the person/s), allow the person/s to approach and talk to you.

■ If you are confident with the situation, they can command your dog to approach them and instruct him to sit.

■ They should reward the dog with a treat or a toy: throw a ball and replace it with a food treat on retrieval.

■ Following this event, they should dismiss your dog.

■ Repeat with different people in different situations. Once your dog begins to show calmness, repeat in your home or garden.

Step 2

■ Ask a friend/s and/or child/children visit your home. Everyone must remain calm and relaxed, and possess clicker and dog treats.

■ Just before the appointed arrival time, recall your dog and make him sit several times in a 'click and treat' session.

■ When your 'arranged actors' arrive, they should only knock on the door or ring the doorbell once at the prearranged time.

■ When, or if, your dog rushes to the door, use the whistle (to signal recall and reward). Use training discs to signal non-reward.

■ Your visitor/s must wait until you're ready (with your dog recalled and sat). Walk to the door with him and praise his calmness.

■ Tell him to 'Sit', and open the door. The visitor/s should enter with a basic greeting and ignore your dog.

■ In your chosen room, tell him to 'Sit' and reward him with a

Training discs

Use these to signal and interrupt problem behaviours. If your dog 'attacks' letters as they are being delivered, ask a person to 'deliver' something as you work on interruption 'recall and reward' methods (clicker and whistle). You can reduce the problem by preventing your dog being 'rewarded' by his behaviour.

Right: *When a visitor comes to the house, make your dog 'sit' and then reward him.*

food treat. Ask the visitor/s to offer him a click and food treat.

■ If successful, everyone must then ignore your dog.

■ If a crating method is used, the dog should stay there until a few minutes before your visitor/s are due to leave. Release him and tell him to sit in front of you and your guests.

■ Some dogs display territorial and/or fear aggression towards visitors when they are leaving. This is because nervous dogs are 'rewarded' by relief after they have 'chased off' the perceived threat or 'intruders'. In these instances, have your dog's favourite toy or a food treat ready to use as a distraction tool. A family member should hold this item whilst another leads the guests away.

■ If re-training alone, go to the door calmly with the reward visible to your dog and tell him to sit at the door while your guests exit. Praise any calm behaviour and reward him with the item and a firm pat and/or a food treat. Patting, stroking, vocal praise or 'click and treat' are all correct responses.

■ Repeat as many times as possible. Eventually, you will retrain your dog and will also make the 'connection' and association between strangers/children and rewarding him.

CHAPTER
SIX

Reducing excitability towards dogs

When your dog is more secure in his environment, start de-sensitizing him from lunging, barking and jumping at other dogs – create a 'controlled' scenario in which he meets them.

Some nervous or dominant dogs are more inclined to display excitability or aggression towards other dogs when they on the lead, perhaps because they are frustrated by being held back from exploring and new encounters, or they may interpret the restricted movement of another dog as 'standoffishness', which equals dominance. The following therapy should be undertaken initially with dogs restrained on short 'simple-strap'-type leads.

Ask a friend who has a 'passive', non-aggressive dog to help with a 'retraining' programme. A 'calm dog' can demonstrate that not all dogs are threatening.

Click and treat training

1 Give your dog an on-the-lead 'control walk' away from the place you have chosen for the encounter. It is important that the territory on which both dogs will be present is neutral. If your dog is powerful and has previously displayed aggression towards other dogs, it is advisable to use a muzzle for reassurance.
2 Encourage your dog to sit, rewarding his obedience with reassurance and a food treat.
3 When the other dog has been brought into view, slacken your hold on the lead and stay relaxed. Any apprehension you feel is transmitted through the lead and by hormonal signals.
4 With your dog under control (sitting), offer a further reward – a treat or toy – as the other dog is walked (side-on) past about 10 m (32 ft) away. Keep your dog sideways-on to the other dog to prevent your dog appearing dominant and provoking the other dog to be aggressive. Click/treat can be offered to your dog as a reward for appropriate behaviour and to aid distraction. Ignore

Above: *With your dog under control, ask a friend to walk past sideways on to your dog. Reward him with a treat and* praise when he responds well and ignores the other dog.

any excited behaviour as your attention can inadvertently reinforce and reward unwanted behaviour. Try other interruption or distraction methods, such as a squeaky toy, whistle linked to a reward, or a ball or treats, to maintain interest and direct control.
5 Gradually decrease the distance between the two dogs.
6 End the session before any excitability or aggression is shown by your dog. Praise him for the appropriate behaviour.

Important
■ These sessions should be repeated as frequently as possible with the distance between the dogs gradually reduced until they can pass within a metre without aggression being shown.

■ Training discs can be used to signal to your dog that he must cease any inappropriate behaviour.

■ Be consistent with the signals you give him. Don't encourage (and praise) him to be a guard dog on one occasion and then be critical on another when he does not welcome other dogs or strangers. You will only confuse him and create more insecurity.

■ Click and treat' good responses and end on a positive note.

Poor recall

As explained earlier, walks represent 'hunting and foraging' episodes to a dog. This is why they become so excited by the prospect and respond to visual and sound behavioural cues, such as putting on coats and rattling keys. Try to reduce these stimuli and make less 'fuss'. Some dominant yet insecure dogs can be stubborn about walks, even refusing them, because they cannot 'control' them. It is normal behaviour for a dog to explore and become excited during walks. You can improve your dog's recall and prevent him chasing and running away if you follow the guidelines below.

Improving recall

1 At home, during a short session in the garden, sound a 'reward whistle', recall your dog and offer a click/food reward for sitting by your side. Repeat five or six times. Follow this sequence, once it has proved successful, with a the retrieval of a favourite toy – frisbees or balls are best – and further success should prove beneficial for training during freestyle walks. Gradually phase out the food rewards over the weeks, substituting praise and a pat.

2 The random use of the 'reward whistle' is essential to change a dog's 'running away' behaviour. If your dog is only recalled during 'exciting events', he will make an association and display the behaviours that you don't want. 'Freestyle' walks can still be enjoyed, but exercise more control. However, during the early

Above: *Practise random recall frequently to get your dog accustomed to coming back to you at your command.*

weeks of re-training it may be better to prevent your dog confronting strangers and retrain him with an extending lead.

Walking in a new area will encourage him to be more responsive to signals. Try distraction methods if he becomes aggressive or excitable. Sound a whistle or squeaky toy, call him to your side and, on his arrival, tell him to 'Sit'. Give him your attention or use a 'clicker' and a significant food reward, such as cooked liver or chicken, or a new toy.

Socializing nervous/aggressive dogs

Nervous dogs may have experienced difficulties during their early socialization period (sometimes because of rescue or re-homing). A rescue dog that has been exposed to confusing changes often shows 'fear aggression' or hyperactivity (excessive barking, etc.) towards other dogs and/or 'territorial aggression' towards strangers. If it has been attacked by other dogs, it may develop a 'get in first' strategy of aggressive behaviour. Unfortunately, stray dogs may have aggressive encounters with other dogs by unwittingly entering their territory. The same is true of dogs that have been/

are being dominated by another dog within the home; they will often display aggression towards dogs they encounter outdoors.

The behaviour of the 'other dog' in outdoor confrontations will often dictate how a 'nervous' dog reacts. If a strange dog approaches your dog and 'stands', licks its mouth and wags its tail (calming signals) without attempting to pick up an anal scent, this behaviour may be interpreted as non-challenging and an invitation to join a chase (forage). However, sometimes the stance will be interpreted as dominance (especially with eye-to-eye contact) and may be considered challenging. If an approaching dog attempts to 'scent' your dog and growls or barks, this can trigger a nervous dog into an aggressive challenge or full fight.

The 'controlled' introduction

Introducing your dog (or re-introducing him) to another of your dogs or a friend's dog needs to be undertaken carefully. Owners will influence some of their dog's behaviour by giving out the wrong signals (through body and chemical languages). Any nervousness or apprehension is signalled through pheromones scent (skin scents) which communicates basic emotions between animals. You can 'reinforce' problem behaviour by giving the 'wrong signal' to a nervous dog. Be positive in your approach and have a 'reward signal' ready and in place for good behaviour – ideally, a whistle signal randomly linked with a food reward.

Introduction should be on 'neutral territory' for all the dogs to focus them on exploring, marking and scenting.

Socialization programme

1 Give all the dogs involved a 'control walk' away from the others. This should consist of at least a 50-m (53-yd) walk which includes five stops, sits, waits and 'walk ons'. Reward good behaviour with a food treat, pat and/or praise.
2 Lead walk the dogs on parallel paths, about 5 m (16 ft) apart.

Interrupt any sign of 'aggression', barking or nervousness with the promise of a play session – show the dog a ball or frisbee – and the smell of the treats. Click and treat all good reactions.

3 If aggression/hyperactive behaviour has not been displayed, simultaneously release the dogs from the lead. Walk them back on a parallel route. Don't encourage physical contact between the dogs and their owners. Use a 'reward whistle' signal to recall the dogs. Tell them to sit, offer a reward, dismiss them and then continue walking. The longer and more varied the walk, the better.

4 When the walk is over and you return to your cars or either owner's house, don't let the dogs enter together. Gate or door thresholds and the rear of vehicles can represent 'competition' triggers. Dogs are best taken separately or crated separately.

5 Socialize the dogs together in the garden following the walk. Do not stand over them, anticipating or expecting aggression. Your physical presence will influence their behaviour!

Above: *After a walk, let the two dogs socialize and play together in the garden while you stay out of the way.*

CHAPTER SEVEN

Healthcare

Prevention is always better than cure, and you can maximize your dog's chances of staying fit and healthy and avoiding many common illnesses and health problems by giving him daily walks, clean water and a varied, balanced diet. A good 'fresh air' walk is healthy for both of you. Sometimes it's good to have a friend who doesn't want to burden you with their problems. A happy, healthy dog will repay you with many years of rewarding obedience and companionship.

I t is a good idea to develop the habit of checking your dog's health in the early days of puppyhood. Begin with a quick inspection of his eyes, ears, mouth, nose, coat, bottom and paws in order to confirm that he is in the peak of condition.

■ Check inside his mouth and make sure that there are plenty of shining, pointed teeth and just a doggy breath rather than a horrible smell. Cleaning his teeth with a special toothbrush and toothpaste a few times a week can be fun for both of you.

■ Excessive discharge from the eyes, blackness or inflammation in the ears and a very dry nose are all early warnings of potential health problems in the future.

■ Excessive hair loss to the coat, signs of soiling on the bottom or limping indicate a need to have your puppy or dog examined.

If you are not sure about any aspect of your dog's health and suspect that there might be a problem, make an appointment for him to see your vet and talk it over with the expert.

CHAPTER
SEVEN

Self-help

There is a lot that you can do on a practical basis to prevent many common health problems without recourse to your vet, especially in preventing flea and worm infestations.

Fleas

Dogs and puppies can easily pick up fleas when they come into contact with other animals. A minor or early sign of fleas, such as excessive scratching or telltale black specks resembling coal dust in the dog's coat, can be treated locally with sprays, powders and collars. However, serious infestations sometimes also require more radical treatment of the animal's environment. Most treatments kill or prevent reproduction but they do not kill the fleas' eggs. It is important, therefore, to use them in conjunction with an indirect spray for skirtingboards, dog beds and carpets. Other pets, such as cats, should also be treated. The best, and most expensive, treatments are applied via a pipette onto the dog's neck and shoulders and are very effective.

Most treatments are effective for up to six months and, ideally, are given at the end of spring and beginning of autumn when parasites benefit from the warmer climate.

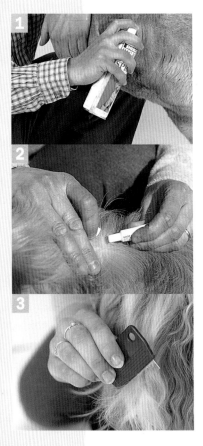

Left: *The most effective way to deal with fleas is preventing them from getting established in your home. This requires regular spraying (1) or applications (2) and combing with a special flea comb (3).*

Walk on the wild side

Be wary of exposing your dog to extremes of terrain and potential contact with dogs or other animals that can carry fleas, mites and ticks. Be sure of 100 per cent recall before releasing your dog onto open moorland or countryside where livestock may be grazing. These animals may be a source of infection. After a walk in the country through bracken and streams, it may be advisable to bath your dog or dry him thoroughly with clean towels and then groom him. This will make it easier to check for any cuts, ticks or fleas and to deal with them quickly.

Worms

Internal parasites can be prevented by simple treatments, and your vet can advise you on these. Tapeworms and roundworms are most common and can cause a range of health problems. A typical symptom is if your dog drags his rear end along the ground. You must worm your dog regularly (usually twice a year for adult dogs; more often for puppies) to protect him.

Ticks

These are usually picked up in the countryside from farm animals, such as sheep. They look like black splinters in the coat and can be dealt with directly by using an anti-tick spray on the affected areas. You can remove the ticks by dabbing the area with alcohol and then carefully pulling them out with tweezers.

Right: *Specialist tick tweezers can be bought at most pet stores. Only use them after the tick has died, usually a few hours after applying anti-tick spray or dabbing alcohol directly onto the tick. Any part of the tick remaining will go septic.*

CHAPTER
SEVEN

SIGNS OF GOOD HEALTH

Your dog should look fit and healthy, be full of energy and always ready for a walk or a game. He should have a consistent, healthy appetite and be the right weight for his size – neither too fat nor too thin. He should urinate and pass stools regularly every day. If his behaviour or appearance is different from normal, watch him closely and if you are worried, check it out with your vet. Changes in temperament or behaviour are often warning signs of present or future health problems.

Signs of poor health

- Sudden weight loss
- Loss of appetite
- Increased thirst
- Vomiting
- Diarrhoea
- Constipation
- Dull coat
- Persistent scratching
- Obsessive licking
- Skin problems
- Pain when moving
- Limping
- Bad breath
- Sore gums
- Dragging the hindquarters
- Loss of energy
- Coughing
- Discharge from
nose and eyes

■ Anal region
Should be clean without any traces of faeces in the fur.

Signs of good health

- Bright eyes
- Shining coat
- Lively trot
- Pricked-up ears
- Damp nose
- Sweet breath
- Wagging tail

Ears
Should be alert and responsive. They should smell pleasant with no visible wax.

Eyes
Should be bright with no signs of discharge or tear stains.

Nose
Should be damp and cold without any discharge.

Mouth
The teeth should be white, smooth – not cracked, broken or yellow. The gums should look pink and healthy, and the breath should not smell unpleasant.

Coat
Should be glossy with no signs of fleas and no sore patches or inflamed skin underneath.

Body
Should be firm, well-muscled and not too thin nor overweight.

Claws
Should not be broken nor too long – they should end level with the pad.

CHAPTER
SEVEN

SIGNS OF ILL HEALTH

As your relationship with your dog develops, you will know more about him than anyone else. Once his rhythms of activity, eating and sleeping have become established, you can expect him to show happy and healthy signs. Should he suddenly experience any changes from his normal behaviour, this may be a sign of a health problem. Temporary changes should not be a cause for alarm but a dramatic change needs to be checked by your vet.

Lack of appetite

If your dog loses his appetite or shows a distinct weight loss, see your vet as quickly as possible. Weight loss can be an indicator of internal parasites, such as worms. It is essential that all puppies and dogs are wormed regularly (see page 117) to protect them. Puppies should be wormed regularly up to four or five months of age and every six months thereafter. Treatments for tapeworm should be given once or twice a year to an adult dog.

Diarrhoea

Puppies with continually loose bowels or extreme diarrhoea are in immediate danger of suffering life-threatening dehydration. You may wish to discuss an early bout of looseness with the breeder. However, if in any doubt, take your puppy to the vet.

The causes of diarrhoea are varied and range from a dietary change to scavenging the wrong items and bacterial infections. It may take time to fight off the debilitating effects of an intestinal infection. Antibiotics will often reduce the natural bacteria needed by the digestive system to break down foods, but offering specific foods can compensate for a biological imbalance. Your vet will be only too pleased to discuss food types with you.

Adult dogs that show signs of long-term looseness or extreme diarrhoea require treatment and possibly a change of diet. Older, less active dogs don't require high-protein foods and will benefit from dietary foods available at good pet shops or veterinary clinics.

Ears

One of the most vulnerable areas in a dog is the outer ear. If infections, such as ear mites – easily identifiable as black specks – or inflammation are not identified early on, these can spread into the middle and inner ear where they are more difficult to treat. Examine your dog's ears regularly for signs of mites, soreness or excessive dirt. The outer ear can be safely cleaned outwards with a cotton ball partly soaked in tepid water.

Above: *You can clean your dog's ears with damp cotton wool.*

Dog breeds with long, floppy ears can be more prone to infections than other breeds. Regular cleaning usually prevents most bacterial infections from taking hold and becoming much more difficult to treat. You can use a dropper to introduce a cleaning oil which can be massaged gently into the ear.

Eyes

If excessive mucus is produced by the eyes (sometimes indicated by a constantly wet area beneath each or one eye), gently wipe the area with a clean cotton wipe, moistened with warm water. Always wipe away from the eyes and the tear ducts, and ensure that the cotton wipe is rinsed clean before wiping again. Better still, use a clean cotton sheet for each wipe. You can irrigate the eye with a weak eye cleaner. Cotton wool should not be used because it is possible to leave traces in the eye. If in any doubt about the seriousness of the problem, consult your vet.

Skin and coat

Your dog's coat can offer a 'quick insight' into his general health. By grooming him regularly, you can identify any areas of extreme hair loss which may indicate a general skin infection.

■ **Mite infections:** patches of bare skin may be signs of various mite infections, known as mange and eczema.

■ **Skin disorders:** these should always be referred to your vet immediately. The sooner that you identify a problem, the easier the infection is to treat.

Below: *Certain breeds, like the West Highland White Terrier, are prone to skin disorders. Check with your vet what you should look for and examine your dog after grooming him.*

When to visit the vet

If the following symptoms occur over a 24-hour period or more, they may indicate that your dog needs an immediate veterinary examination. Any abnormal breathing or bleeding from a large wound, the mouth, nose, genitals or anus should also be regarded as a health problem. Although the symptoms listed may indicate a specific disorder, they are not necessarily indicative of that particular health problem. Your vet will diagnose what is wrong and advise on a course of appropriate treatment.

Signs of ill health

Signs of intestinal infections and Parvovirus
- Diarrhoea (for more than a day) and continual vomiting
- Visible inflammation (redness) or discharge in the eyes or ears
- Discoloured faeces
- Weight loss
- Vomiting (may also indicate poisoning if accompanied by collapse, twitching, etc.)

Signs of parasite infection or dermatological allergy
- Excessive scratching
- Baldness

Signs of eye infections, e.g. conjunctivitis and glaucoma
- Discharge
- Redness
- Inflammation and/or swelling
- Blocked tear ducts
- Grey coating and cataracts
- Third eyelid exposed (in some breeds this is normal)

Signs of major organ disease or diabetes
- Listlessness
- Eye discolouring
- Loss of appetite
- Weight loss
- Excessive thirst and drinking of water

Signs of seizure, heart disease or airway blockage
- Convulsions
- Excessive coughing

Visiting the vet

If it is difficult to control your dog in the surgery, leave him in the car and ask the nurse to advise you when it is time to have him ready. Introduce him to your vet by name and explain the problems or any queries you may want answered.

Nursing a sick dog

While nursing your dog, try not to fuss too much as your distress may compound any disorientation he is experiencing. Keep him in a quiet place, stay calm and always use a low-toned voice to reassure him.

Administering medicine

Dogs may be less complex than children in terms of behaviour and intelligence but they share the same aversion to medicine!

■ **Tablet treatments** may need to be disguised in tasty titbits, such as soft meat.

Above: If your dog won't take a tablet disguised in a titbit, place the tablet in the back groove of the mouth, then hold the mouth closed and gently rub the throat.

■ **Liquids** are best applied directly into the mouth via a syringe. Insert it at the side of the mouth onto the back of the tongue. Ask someone to hold the dog's head and keep his body still between their knees while you administer the liquid.

■ **Ear drops and eye drops** may need two people to administer as dogs can squirm free of the tightest grips. Eyes can be irrigated using weak, cold tea or a teaspoon of boracic acid solution in a cup of lukewarm water. Use a dropper to administer the solution, which flushes out unwanted objects such as hair or dust.

Above: *Use a dropper to flush out any foreign bodies in the eye, then very gently massage the liquid in.*

The correct approach

Note: Always be positive and confident in your approach when administering treatments and have everything you need ready in advance. The faster the treatment is given, the better. Your dog will be as relieved as you that his dignity has been restored.

CHAPTER
SEVEN

FIRST AID

Many common accidents, as well as more serious emergencies, will require first aid. Although you can treat some minor injuries yourself, if you are ever in doubt, you should seek veterinary help immediately. It could make all the difference to your dog's health.

Sprains

Large dogs can easily sprain a leg muscle when they're bounding about. Apply a cold compress (old cotton sheeting doused in cold water) immediately to the area, and then twice every hour thereafter. After several applications, replace with a warm-water compress to encourage blood flow in the muscle.

Cuts and wounds

Any cuts, wound damage or splinters to the pads on the paws should be bathed before treating.
■ **Splinters:** gently remove with tweezers. Use a mild antiseptic bath to help prevent secondary infection. An old sock can be put on the dog's foot to prevent him licking the affected area.
■ **Simple cuts and scratches:** these can happen on adventurous walks. Wash them twice daily for about a week with some cotton wool soaked in a mild antiseptic diluted in warm water.
Note: The same can be applied to mild insect bites.

Choking

This must be addressed carefully in dogs. Open the jaws wide to locate the obstruction or place the dog over your shoulder and lightly pat him like a baby to dislodge the object.

Convulsions

These may be the result of an epileptic seizure. In this instance, place the dog in a quiet, dark room and give him time to recover before taking him to the veterinary clinic for examination.

Poisoning

If you suspect your dog has come into contact with a poisonous solution, immediately wash him off completely in case there is any residue on his coat, head or limbs. This is important should he continue to lick off the pollutant.

If you suspect that he has swallowed a poisonous substance, encourage him to vomit by using an emetic, such as baking soda or warm salty water. However, this is only useful immediately after the event. Take him to the vet immediately. If you are aware of the contaminant, take it with you so the vet can formulate a suitable treatment.

Burns

Simple burns should be doused immediately in ice-cold water. Gently pat dry and rub an antiseptic cream or non-greasy baby's nappy cream into the burn. Your dog will attempt to lick it off but you can make a temporary cardboard funnel collar to prevent excessive licking. If in doubt, seek veterinary advice. Serious burns should be examined and treated by a vet immediately.

Above: *Minor burns must be drenched with ice-cold water immediately.*

CHAPTER
SEVEN